3-

## Also by Laura Moriarty

*An Air Force* (Hooke Press, 2007)
*Ultravioleta,* a novel (Atelos 2006)
*Self-Destruction* (Post-Apollo 2005)
*Nude Memoir* (Krupskaya 2000)
*Cunning,* a short novel (Spuyten Duyvil 1999)
*The Case* (O Books 1998)
*Spicer's City* (Poetry New York 1998)
*Symmetry* (Avec 1996)
*L'Archiviste* (Zasterle 1991)
*Rondeaux* (Roof 1990)
*like roads* (Kelsey St. Press 1990)
*Duse* (Coincidence Press 1986,
reprinted Paradigm Press 1999)
*Persia* (Chance Additions 1983)
*Two Cross Seizings* (Sombre Reptiles 1980)

# *A* Semblance

# *A* Semblance

## Selected and New Poems:
### 1975-2007

## Laura Moriarty

OMNIDAWN PUBLISHING
RICHMOND, CALIFORNIA
2007

Cover Image: Photos by Laura Moriarty on photo album page.

Book cover and interior design by Ken Keegan.

Offset printed in the United States on archival, acid-free recycled paper
by Thomson-Shore, Inc., Dexter, Michigan

Omnidawn Publishing is committed to preserving ancient
forests and natural resources. We elected to print *A
Semblance* on 50% post consumer recycled paper, processed
chlorine free. As a result, for this printing, we have saved:

6  Trees (40' tall and 6-8" diameter)
2,388  Gallons of Wastewater
960  Kilowatt Hours of Electricity
263  Pounds of Solid Waste
517  Pounds of Greenhouse Gases

Omnidawn Publishing made this paper choice because our
printer, Thomson-Shore, Inc., is a member of Green Press
Initiative, a nonprofit program dedicated to supporting
authors, publishers, and suppliers in their efforts to reduce
their use of fiber obtained from endangered forests.

For more information, visit www.greenpressinitiative.org

Library of Congress Catalog-in-Publication Data

Moriarty, Laura.
   A semblance : selected and new poems : 1975-2007 / Laura Moriarty.
      p. cm.
   ISBN 978-1-890650-27-8 (trade pbk. : alk. paper)
   I. Title.
   PS3563.0871635S46  2007
   811'.54--dc22

                                                            2007023641

Published by Omnidawn Publishing, Richmond, California
   www.omnidawn.com    (510) 237-5472    (800) 792-4957
              10  9  8  7  6  5  4  3  2  1

ISBN:  978-1-890650-27-8

# Acknowledgments

"Spectrum's Rhetoric," from *A Tonalist* appeared in *Sal Mimeo #5*, Fall 2004.
"Welcome Dear Chaos," from *Divination* appeared in *The New Review*.

Thanks to the editors and to the publishers of Sombre Reptiles, Chance Editions, Coincidence, Kelsey St., Roof, Zasterle, Avec, Poetry New York, O Books, Spuyten Duyvil, Paradigm, Krupskaya, Post-Apollo, Atelos, and Hooke Press also thank you.

# Contents

# Introduction:

# Notes to an Allegory of Song

> "I was interested in song and in the persuasive powers of song, the powers of repetition and the powers of convention."
> Laura Moriarty, interviewed by Standard Schaefer, *New College Review*

Allegory carries a second meaning along with the surface story or song. It is a structural principle that conceals as it reveals. Writing is both action and imitation of action. Within elements of meaning or thought it represents ideas (or sounds, or rhythms).

*allos*, other, the other
*agoreuein*, to speak

To speak of the other as a technique of literature is self-critical to begin with. In *A Semblance*, Laura Moriarty speaks the "Allegory of song" ("Cryptophasia" from *Self-Destruction*) and, by analogy, "song" can stand in for just about anything. Analogy has its own set of binding limitations, but Moriarty's writing explodes with intention in every direction, registering her principal themes and poetics: love, war, serendipity, fate, memory, death; masque, hyperbole, latency, *saudade*, fragment, sentence, melody, harmony, lyric and anti-lyric, repetition (delayed, suspended, elaborated), determining, and undermining.

> "I tell everything in plain words
> Thinking against the action"
> Moriarty, "That explode together," *Symmetry*

15

Thinking against the action, as opposed to action. But you are stopped by something, a thought, the realization that action can be thinking, thinking is a kind of action. In the poetics of proprioception, Charles Olson ("Proprioception") writes, *"movement or action/ is 'home.'"* So "against" could in this case be a collision, a contrast, a comparison, a partial payment, collusion. Or a resting in relation to, a something given in exchange for something else. And like the tales of Scheherazade, or Shahrazada, the Persian queen who knew all the poets "by heart," the "against" is everything likely to be given in exchange for life or death.

Moriarty's early chapbook *Duse*, like Arthur Rimbaud's "Le bâteau ivre," is the model for her future works. *Duse* sets up a table of apparent verticals side by side, but reads down and across, and then begins to spiral every which way, a kind of *diagramming* which threads through *A Semblance*, forming and reforming phonemes, words and phrases, thoughts and tales, rhythm and sound.

> "Loss as rest from meaning"
> Moriarty, *Duse*

Loss could be failure, bereavement, privation, or deprivation. Rest could mean remainder as well as reminder, or rest as balance. The rest in music is the stop-gap, accentual, creating time, or holding back the next (imminent) sound, or dwelling on the tones of what was just heard. Rest is also balance, scale, a leveling out, but it will implicate excess, death. Being in balance is precarious, a nanosecond away from destruction, a haunting self-destruction. Song breathes the haunting, at times, "a feeling of nostalgia, a sense at once of fulfillment and loss" (Husain Haddaway, translator of *The Arabian Nights*). From the Portuguese *fado*, the urban folk song of destiny, love, and betrayal, arises *saudade*, yearning for unrealized dreams, the homesickness for a place perhaps you haven't yet seen. And meaning is the game.

> "games of chance, divinatory procedures, memory and fate"
> Moriarty, "Memory & Fate: The Game"
> *The New Review*

The game is the frame. "Is the frame holding?" asks Lily (Angelica Huston) in *The Grifters*." "Yes," answers her son Roy (John Cusack) just before she inadvertently kills him. A frame or grid is a binding structure Moriarty uses to "go out of bounds," her theatricality "telling everything in plain words."

"These are facts."
Moriarty, *The Case*

Among her many "others" are Conan Doyle, Laurie King, James Ellroy, Ian Rankin, Neal Stephenson, and William Gibson, as well as the poets, musicians, filmmakers and artists, especially Blake, Schuyler, Niedecker, Brathwaite, Halsey and Duchamp. The diagrams, the representation of subject as puzzle, the noir features imagine "the transitory, the fugitive, the contingent" (Baudelaire, 1859 definition of modernity), modernism, the objective nature of the work.

The frame is always involved in "circling and mirroring" (Mary Douglas, *Thinking in Circles: An Essay on Ring Composition*), figuring the limits of its excess, going beyond yet always coming to terms, its terms: the past-future-nowness, the just-before or just-after, the fact of its happening in language imagining reality; the plural realities that could have had…or been…; parts in relation to a whole or holes. Its purposeful disorder is rupture marking the forms that melt into one another.

Like veils of light on water, Moriarty's delicate materiality of wordwork is synaesthetic, tone as color and sound. Writing references experience—here—and here—as palimpsest, markings, the traces recording tiny gestures coming together or breaking apart at the surface and in space, inner or outer, in 3-D. All her writings "can be seen as an autobiographical marker, a cue, by which I evoke a moment from my past, or my projected future, each a charm to conjure a mental reality and to give it physical form" (Mary Heilmann, *The All Night Movie*). From her pasts or projected futures, memory in its formal status as the written does not have to be nostalgic unless Moriarty clearly wants it.

What she chooses is to frame and to disrupt the framing structures of language, memory, imagery, history, with clear-eyed humor, in order to inhabit new possibilities, new lamps for old, as Aladdin says, while claiming both, supporting the frame as a perpetual state of becoming.

> "There were no equivalents"
> Moriarty, "La Malinche," *Rondeaux*

Deferments, beginning and beginning again. Lines are longer than they appear. Lean lines grow fatter with dreams, untold parts, partnerings, partings, the allegories of becoming, rhapsodic études of love and war, as in the prose poem "Pure Lyric" from *Self-Destruction*. "Like pure war a politics and architecture." As Tyrone Williams signals, "the lyric impulse can still serve as a site for social [and political] criticism." As Laura Moriarty says in her blog A Tonalist Notes (atonalistdoc. blogspot.com) "international but local, like yourself."

Each new poem furthers the context for all poems. A volatile critical lyric employs her, occupies her. Using pitch as a register to key words with worlds, Moriarty's acute gesture is the corresponding song that becomes allegory.

Norma Cole

# *A* Semblance

# Waking from
# Sleep a Thousand Miles Thick

The blue crack as the snow
Unfastens the house
Sheer moon section white leaf
eyes beaming drip
with salt-heavy
silver coin sleep
Heated air tired
seeps out of flesh
I wake each morning velvet
eared from night's wine
Listen for the child
Our animals nestling
Count themselves mumble
Calm stars fading
Energy bristles from tight
Foreheads, eyes
Violet shadows like spirits
Leap between house and barn
The day's whir begins
The sun's lip
enfolds the horizon

Blouse crumpled my
breasts unbuttoned into sleeping
lips The spirits handspring October
white apple smell nostril
quivers Sugar taste
The dream pours into the listening
room Petals bunch into
eyes closed against stark
light golden, speeding Our room

winged mother-of-pearl within its
tough clam bright car merging
onto a swift freeway at dawn

Using 44 words from
Bruce Conner's "Tables and Cards"
Hansen-Fuller Gallery, Nov. 1975

# From *Persia*

# Persia

a woman much withered, a maid
a maiden with a wand a handsome
maid, white wand with a peacock of
solid gold on its tip

who did you meet?

an elaborate design where the surrogate
parents never encounter the biological

yet she retains
the above

sensation of malaise
after ascending

spread out inevitably blue

In the moments before loss of consciousness
he surveyed the panel with exaggerated calm
apparently in slow motion

she's breaking up

the giant's explanation
uncontrolled increase or
diminishing in an arithmetical
sequence of circles
water

water falling

discovered in the bucket
I smell the blood

minimal needs of consciousness
(shown in broken lines)

voice     approach
flight

an urgent appeal

ending as usual

reduced to a point of contact

#

Oriental as in orientation
chromatic succession a list of reds

mirage

typically "our magi"
"our mystics" as those here considered

a blackened corona was enough

has drawn him north though he has
lived there already and there he will
pick fruit The orchards are endless
It's autumn

an act of existing which

as a nostalgia for green
for something purely green

28

multiplication not

here is a diagram

an accomplice, needless to repeat,
who is identical

to see things tending that way meaning
up, as in the old trick of looking up

identical with (not) being able to focus

as the foci of an ellipse

is one diagram of this situation

#

there is a hidden man

He also experiences increasing powerlessness
due to fatigue, forgetfulness and disgust

Unfortunately, would he not therefore fall into
the trap of this invented and complacently
accepted picture of this situation?

The Day whose constraints are deplored

insects made of light (evening knowledge)

to recognize the prehistoric birds
as insects made of light

in that the window spoken of by a certain
sufi may be a source of light or an

individual a source of shadow capable of
projecting itself

as further a thing may be made invisible
by an excess (lack) of light

we need a diagram

a wooden machine that makes the sound of birds

of birds while grinding everything to dust

he left his tools behind when he
installed the window

look up

again a man arrives on a plane
the only other thing in this picture is sand

an indigence amounting to inessence

he's not here


*persia*


near here
but as we've read
filled with ash

mouth The mouth
in this case meaning north

We were found in his car

# X.  The Tenth Card

Discovered a traitor in my home

a statuette also me
a defender of the heart

Don't let unexpected situations 'throw' you

Far too many

Is one fortune like another?

since ancient Greeks wagered on the turn
of a shield on the point of a sword. Today

A false turning
When he said

I believed you was doing me wrong
And now I know

#

Heart disease isn't
as simple as it sounds

If possible
There is a shortness of breath

In the subtractive
color wheel

There is draining
as in a wound

In a wound
there is too much talking

You arrive full
and leave empty

Announcing that passion
brings suffering

or something equally
banal

But who would believe a thief?
Who would?

#

A trap is laid
or a tramp

is a wanderer
Losing the bright

Never finally "true to life"

A color thief
also a magician

substitutes contrast
for accuracy

Human will however
is never enough

# six histories

My entire forget
not thought to have him
turn me to hope again

Pinned his sweater above
his breast to have him
again the hollow there

Medal to him pricked well
below his shoulder
thought to have him there then

One entire piercing
me hard thoughts for once
for to me they're both him

Again he turns to him
for me not caring
to hope my thoughts over

Pinned to some shoulder turned
away my breast again
entirely him

From *like roads*

# 8 barriers

illuminate and choose


a room turns into a door

it's about to pour this canyon

is shaped like a drain

an alley suddenly the spigot

your canteen overflown to channels

engraved on each foot

girlish hands have smoothed our

paper thin walls like air


like roads exude


identification corrosive or spat

as you sat a marginal man over

head new in town a new town

prearranged a transparent line

fastens each corner to the sun

alters the scale the intervening

distance shrinks to a runway

a ramp built like a hot motel


we sign the wall


they point at your face when

asking where to go the centipede

blocks all the way shallow

receptacles ground into a lens

Is this a wall or a secretion?

Being Sifted the hero remains in the past


this unnamed ruin


(windows) was excavated including

centuries of practical unconsciousness

engineers didn't know they existed

a sequence of activities

as for example the knots you taught

off-handedly which knowing already

not its physicality but the reason

behind each knot you had intended


satellite communities


our teeth worn to the quick

barely visible furrows a tribute

to the manufacture of bones for space

the book of what is water

opens to a tainted corridor often

uncovered we long for its breadth

like every visitor puzzled by doors

as if entering were a formula


we climb into a room


outside a road designed for a glittering

parade a question whose answer

straightness so that the landscape is felt

as obstructive and later invisible

when dissolved the neighborhood

and crockery so we agreed to leave

by all walking the same way only

our skins cracking like the pots we sat on


but weren't we all crazy then?


ignoring the spiders in the water

negative spaces closing in that earlier

talk of freedom becoming concrete

perimeters pavilions decoys theft

I was as guilty as anyone or we

all had our little sayings though


sights forgotten this way


draw the borders from their shells

it's calming to be in the main room

but to go that slow you must let the idea

solidify around you much as a map

disembodies yet renders significant

features which may otherwise be mistaken

perhaps for pain or for a storm arranging

itself yet another range of hills

# From *Rondeaux*

Each page a day
Each rectangle outlined
On the sky there is movement
We are under it it is raining
These days remembering back
To that day actually the present
Streets meeting already writing
As if divided I write you and see
Each page handing it over directly
You at the same time in a speech
Make writing into life
Paper in hair and eyes
Mixed with the general storm
Inundated with each other
Each page says anything

Naked still on the second day
A current goes through my handwriting
My diary overcome the sea
Is like silk today There is
An unusual situation with us and the sun
And the moon big on the horizon
This is the story of the birth of Diana
Of your creation of a lover on paper
Naked but keeping track I write
To wish the season upon you
From the middle of my life to the middle of yours
In this rude outdoor existence exposed
Writing that I realized I missed the floods
As they pulled away revealing only mud long covered
Naked at last again as I write this

As I taste it's warm almost hot
If quiet I can hear as well as see
A woman chopping celery in a bright
Kitchen from the back window
But she doesn't see me watching
Her movements are precise and quickly
She has everything laid out One must
Learn how to cook or how to drink tea
As I taste as if I were made
Only of the ability to taste
As if I were taught to stop with tea
And to wait to turn on the lights
By one whose experience retains heat
Like a day that was warm or a cup
As I taste it seems to stay hot

Aye, rarely said But you have said
When long When days have gone on
A week spent and leaning against
Some booth or bar say Aye and stop
Not for yes or always though yes always
You put a word to a long even
Breath I have heard you say
With some awe at the slowness of time
Aye, rarely said But you so often
Offer this equivalent for sighing
Named for a vote or forever
Each day a law that passes finally
You number yourself in the tally
You make a perfect total with your
Aye, rarely said But I have heard you say

Let's stay or you said go
Someone running not unusual
To have to go to work at dawn
Glad for the job happily gone
So let them take our places
And not as we did go but stay
An hour completely red not
Reckless though unearthly
Let's stay you were so
Flushed the way a night will
Make you vague and permeable
Nonsense that you or I should be
En route Look someone running
Away and not unhappy to
Let's stay but you said no

Though you complain about your bruises
Among cushions even here even you might find
Some edge to fall apparently against my will
Though not everything is as soft as I am
And not every impulse toward sympathy
Needed or received or not each attempt
To fit a plug into the wall doesn't explode
In your hand and wounds will come
Though you can hide them well enough
You complain meaning I do since it was
You said that though no one else heard
Nothing can be proved but for those bruises
Which even as you complain are both
More and less than you deserve to have and
Though you have them now are fading

Why am I divided from him?
A continuous line begins with the brow
And becomes the nose by agreement
A piece of linen simplifies
The features of its women like
Masks or any other kind of quiet
A beautiful arrangement by convention
Only if accepted or if not
Why am I divided thoughtlessly?
A stylized head bisecting two scenes
Of life or its embroidered equivalent
House man clouds a child suspended from
Parentheses that by balancing unite and yet
Why am I silent in the foreground divided?

And to brave clearness I'd have given
Almost what I did give Nothing
That wasn't strictly speaking mine
Wanting only what was blatant
Giving into the available restraints
With the same passion I might
Have resisted or perhaps I did
For it was the same damn thing
And too brave or too grand for anything
Like what I should have done or been
All things reduced to the absence of these
Same things They rush me to return
On time or even before I've gone and said
Here is to all we are not lamenting
And to brave clearness or to what we have instead

# Laura de Sade

"To wear binding like binding" she wrote
Also "my name as the title shows
Is Laura" a common enough situation
To be bound as oneself to admit
To unpardonable pride or unusual
Desires "to court sensuosity as if it were
The judge of truth" as its own renouncing
Stands against men in the old sense
To wear down in the arena
Of full view the libertine regalia
Imagined upon a rigorous silence
As when turning back to a woman
Entangled in leaves an animate
Becomes a sentient piercing willfully
"To where a man's heart beating…"

# La Malinche

Money was anything that came to hand

        She had lips for his eyes

(a violent forgetting that forced return)

Because there was no electricity

        A man fucked

Because there was no water

        A woman from behind

The children passed into the train.

She was spent

The iron money of the Spartans

We wished we were already there.

        Pressed between them

Black inside the train. The landscape was red. In the dark sacristy the heavy lace and peculiar smell of holy water.

The green cross of the Inquisition set into the local pink stone.

The circulation of money

The water was infused with a way of life

Or buried

Yes I know it the Tacuba. Green and black light. Pink and green frosting like stone.

The one you don't want to lose

"Of the Series of Masked Aggressions"

Black tea with heated cream in copper.

Or blending with the street where

The lions. Blue tiles. The House of the Inquisitor has balconies which fly over the street.

As official interpreter she put his orders in the form of rhetorical suggestions tinged with irony.

He put himself inside her mind

Surrounded by souls. A hundred men in black and silver costumes play as they scream.

She had lips painted gold.

On the day of the burning everything was draped in green.

Charged with being enlightened.

They close around him

The dark air of the city. She was forbidden to come. There is always a red zone. It means nothing.

Even if "understanding" here means "destroying"

The sound of *geodas*

A white flower pitcher sells itself. The weaving machine in the hotel Goya. The carriage carries us through the trouble which is black and blue.

            Were thighs made unstable

Those who take on the manners of foreigners

            Because beaten or flattered

The Annunciation here retitled Temptation of the Virgin.

He would do.

The twisted train on its back. Corn spills out. A dark woman in her best dress is transparent.

These romantic landscapes also contain elements of desire, skepticism and anguish.

We found them buried in the remains of the river.

They call him by her name.

            From inside a shudder

But coins were not the first money.

The monkey put

We meet again for ices. The color is poison.

"Cortez's Henchmen Contemplating the Demons of the New World"

The dead people at the edge of town. The play in the language of the conquerors.

A Saint signed by the Treasurer. Every day there was new money.

Because there was no water

       She took it

There were no equivalents

The glass coins of Egypt, the knife money of China

       She had enough

She had lips for his eyes
A man fucked
A woman from behind
Pressed between them
Or buried
The one you don't want to lose
Or blending on the street where
He put himself inside her mind
She had lips painted gold
They close around him
Were thighs made unstable
Because beaten or flattered
From inside a shudder
She took it
She had enough

Duse

Loss as rest from meaning.


To save the theater, the theater must be destroyed,
the actors and actresses must all die of the plague.
It is said in my repertoire I have not created any
new personage. This I consider my best eulogy.

the dead city

the prose theater

elongated

"smashed with a fist the inner
mirror"

inevitable weighted with
or character when believed

we

in your small room          She used this to mean phrase
                            the world a man a line I always
                            always felt that she meant that
                            she filled


                            there time was hours only

one chair with

inlaid with                    In wrapped and later was found
                               to be a whole something gone
                               something else missing

was a slave


table

broken

I lived

destroys not only                    the hotel emblematic which place
                                      was not as now the dead city but
                                      acting was exterior to

small room

this return

your


pine

letters had

stood straight then        life as if she'd had it Wishing
                           to have been at sea I would have


naked
                           "I do you wrong — it's like dying"
marked


bits of

that child

dizzy with            took a switch to her legs so
                      that she entered she as
                      early knowing that whenever
                      the text permitted real cries

there was
                      fell mute

We in bliss pay so

baby

I yes I had

woman was that            women

If                        I gave you those

but I

and felt what she

though I she

dead

sick

              a thousand times until in a
              blackened city weakened

strapped

              by having been born on the road
              "asleep with love"

her legs

              "with absent air living in falsehood
              guilt, crime, alarm, terror"

with excessive

Voices when walking on once
the familiar

with

expires                    script remaining

unkind                     place

stairs                    It's useless to say were words used
                          as and I'm in love with going (it
                          was a play) but was beaten then

crowd into mind

for          what becomes of a thing that
             present heavy with its fact of
             must be done something
             touch so that sense flares
             but actual the weight
             in your hands now entire
             that so long each act was in so
             the longest one time that standing
             what becomes my whole
             and broken not without
             no belief that among was gone
             or when that kind speech
             came for only the only
             but is there is not rest but
             what becomes can we then we

there are days

of ropes and pulleys that
tableau descending so sudden
Convinced them waiting even in
the halls but we

when?

when

costume in


pinned back          So wanting with to feel see
                     not only this

he liked             remembering words


back

my

the form of

       and said I Eleanora and then
       more than ever I knew she was
       not herself I think I fooled
       them I've said remember that
when the play       I existed


pale              they

you lifting

       which place was not

for

white seeds          on the beach after strewn


tin
                     things cherished a whole
leaf                 civilization artificially would
                     have


                     was more like

to serve to


reenact                    By the curtain and the step
                                  there levels transparent only
                                  second nature by then I lived
                                  and breathed that almost that
have not spoken been     woman I was


for

breathe out

hanged

Praise for that tearing stopped
from strangers who don't

as hold that

as they pulled and squeezed

in

the sound

out

scraps torn wrapped

around

and threads

falling it

Covered the walls with my with
something like that was my face

if not then

           my dear that we lived that was
           and faithful to couldn't know
           matter now

stranger


oh stranger        and because I had



           that one he

gallant was


gent                    Life divided so that the
                        parts the parts you see


far



though

chest

opened of               these this to explain her own
                            had nothing unnamed to do with
                            not to not have

pulled clothes torn

from cradles as if         that interweaving planned

we                             can't

was cloth


left                    them burnt


shreds as by


is                       the play

From *L'archiviste*

These were the inhabitants of the city

A man in red a collaborator but

The story was intact

His face clouded

They inhabited the technique

Or he was a thief

A girl makes mistakes

But was distracted by his hand on her cheek

The history of which

The back of his hand

but the planes flattened as they were against remembered variations in
blue fading into yellow at the horizon and then the black returning

Placed them

was like that of history itself. The desire to preserve what was by its nature always lost. The moment of concentration prepares a range of beginnings. There are too many. Some are lists of themselves proceeding back into a claustrophobic infinity. And there are real corridors where a man might squat hidden.


It was a fruit a medicine a drink a stain


                    A dark spill


whose instruments hopelessly entangled


                    Surges of electricity


It was no good to go back in time


                    Gave him certain rights over her


Proof that the animal


The authorities paled turning into cranes


And proudly indoor gardens, elevated trains and walkways


                    He has been around

The machines were lovely

As long as he was going forward

The archivist was helpless in the face of knowledge

There was too much

The new train goes to the ocean. Everything is enclosed in silver. The streamlining slips through nature. These old designs were never realized. Riding in the train she felt pressed into the seat as if reentering a gravitational field. But this was a modern train and her feelings simply sexual obsession.

Which derailed became pure architecture

This was the first of the obscure cities

Luxurious but simple its organization attempted to accommodate the beautiful idea. A government was appointed with strangely limited powers. The members reached beyond their capacities. Massacre was the word used for the times which came. A man without eyes presided.

In a monotone the color of the local sea

Surrounding him on three sides

Misunderstanding could be turned to escape

                              The document was damaged

Injury was only a disguise

But readable

A still wave because in some sense representation but in this case as enfolding as nature. Sits at her desk or is thrown over it. There is no violence in his violence.

From the open ocean these things came and it was known the origin to be irresistible but temporary. Again the word was damage.

or it was said the image refuses itself. Was therefore the research justifiable? The architecture seemed about to embark.

Only the tip of the city was visible.

                              He could and did play anything.

But there was nothing to indicate either the period or the purpose of the monument.

90

The room which doesn't

exist legally has the simple organization of the abandoned fact.

The creatures which light the ocean one would mistake for air around here are always hungry. They can be swallowed or absorbed through the eyes. There is no other defense.

My pocket she said was picked

In Brussels the new town. The light is painted on. The white tower prefigured the existing structure. Bureaucracy accumulating means that there is no location for this city. One carries its edicts, diagrams, licenses, wills, telegrams, warnings. Its shredded evidence. Like a confection on the dark brick. The conductor's blood red hat makes him visible in the green air.

Or the place by its blackness

But it was in the line of cities reduced to an itinerary by the draw of the border with its imagined safety. Money was lost in the exchange and then lost again in the purchase of useless tickets included here. The archivist eyes them evaluatively. She is not the same man anymore.

On arriving at the palace

Having gone through the sixteen stations with the endless stone stairs and arched corridors almost the same each time. I have felt like this before but I was a child then.

The labyrinth of paper made it impossible to stay. There was a feeling of vertigo when stepping over the model of the city. It was all that was left of the fair.

tower of plain light

already infamous. He claimed no one could see him work. The regimentation allowed him to hate the past for the prison that it was.

Because the gray and black and white was all the more against the always wet columns of the interior zones.

Fierce beings indicate the directions

It would not

stay the way he had it figured out.

Then in red or whatever he

known to be at large. He said.

Are you waving the flag at me? Now called fathers and little mothers but they took down the tower. And were killed for anything.

But this graceless city is only a detour.

We weren't visible in our roles

                              unspoken by him

The insistent unspeaking

into the real city beneath our feet

                    or a knife used

smoothly because of his hands which have had what they would.

                    The pages like rain

# From *Spicer's City*

# Golgonooza

Where the explosion leaves off. Where the woman from the other story
the child the refugee coincide. This is the story of a conversation.

my darling the sun

I have already paid

She did she has he said she is but I made him say it. This city is a
garden. A pit. A forest.

We believe

The disguise helps us to release our passions. And then we don't believe
it any more. Fish can be caught with a vegetable bait concocted from
manioc and bitter orange which has been left to rot. Silver tarnished
and rusted.

Symbolic or even creative of violence. But what could we have done?
The angel at the gate. These are the headlines today. We wait for the
war. Anticipation resolves into fulfilled desires.

in the shape of a horse

We want that clear road. The horizon on its back before us. There is a
new interest in toads, vipers, nitric acid, mercury, horror. All is poison.
Nothing is poison. (Paracelcus) He is the Mad Apothecary. What has
he given me? Can I take all of these?

she spoke sweetly

I have visited this island which is like a large convex shield floating in the sea. The poisoner opens a school. He has the eyes of Bela Lugosi in *White Zombie*. A world in which Man is by his nature the enemy of Man. Satan's book of accusations open on his lap.

Mary he began

What is said is particular. It is a language without endings. By use of certain tendencies. He tenders me. I recognized her thighs as she went by on her motorcycle. She crouched into it. A person can be taken for a place or a thing. Babylon's lament. He said. I have made that mistake myself.

persuasion

Love is not the allegory of communication. Sugar is like sand. The allegory of money changes you into me. The passage of Diana and Callisto. Passed out for free. Turns one into a tree. The other into an animal. The tableau of the stranger. He prints it by hand. Mary read it again he says.

Talk of love

Or of civic music as for example by Rubens. What has it to do with me? Things covered in gold. The fiddles like locusts. The museum of the new empire. We are entering another age. Nothing so much as authenticity subjectivity quality. The gallery of the horseman. It was called unedited or natural glass. It was clear and black. The new elite. The night.

rolls back in his skull

not like a real doctor

I look into the yellow eyes of a cat drunk with rum. The moon is almost full and is the same color as the goat at the bottom of this hill. There are too many flowers here. I know women like that. I can look across the miniature bay and see where I've been. It's not like anything. The lights come on and I wonder how it could be so hot.

Expectations (the goat is folded in sleep already) are like the rain forests clinging to the volcanoes around here. Temporary like nostalgia. As if the thing could be active.

The conversation takes

a terrible turn

He called it the Third World War. One version of the future. He wrote a book called *The World*. There Babylon is builded in the Waste, founded in Human desolation. O Babylon (he said) thy Watchman stands over thee in the night. Thy severe Judge all the day long proves thee thy heart's desire.

stolen without shame

changed

The animals of that city have invaded me and I have brought them here. How many miles are in those kilometers? How many times can something be divided? In this equation or in that box of poison it takes ten snakes to make a leopard. It is you I call for or want.

without hesitation

All is poison. Nothing is left. Silver heals itself. Sold to a rapacious clientele. I have already paid. I have already told you. I have opened the window against the dusk.

She explains her love

The animals are imprisoned. We are them. We have always known it. The golden chapel appears on the radio along with a hurricane. A white-line etching painted with watercolors. The rum tasted different when people died to make it. Things are sweet here.

The unity we construct every day can be torn to shreds or split in two. The use of persons is at stake. It is a formalized madness with recognized entities into which the subject changes. There is an incomplete form, expressed roughly in a cry, an unconscious movement. But he was not a skeptic in daily life.

                                renegade that he was

An indescribable anguish took hold of me and I went toward him, putting away the book. The hysteric lies with his body. I knew but didn't say. An adroit counterfeit of language which is like walking on fire.

                            an interminable exchange

Concerning the poisons of the Borgias, so rich in ptomaines. Acid falls on the shoulders and turns you to stone. Fortunately that tree is less common than before. I've been traveling since sunset and I've lost my home.

                            the lamb's death

                            without term

Given a pine torch. We say physiognomy of you. This is not you alone. This is me. When one of these physical elements begins to act independently, we lose possession of ourselves. We have done.

                            is in its nature

An angel whispering reaches through, his hand hovering over her belly.

If you could do something. But having understood everything, or having exhausted the system of names, they encounter only the excessive, the incredible. And how much do we owe you? You give what you like. A long silence grows in which each person is trying to think faster than the other. But the real grammar preceded that calculus.

I have given up my heart

So that the form of it is like a library. Not any library but the one that burned leaving the shape of itself, its foundations overgrown. A new café or shanty or bar built precariously close to the sea.

how can I say

We did not meet old fantasies but only the dissolution of a fantasy. But why was I able to consider myself caught in spells, or what comes to the same thing, in the discourse of witchcraft?

come softly

Including silence, slips of the tongue, repetitions, hesitations and so on. That kind of work is hell. You have to fight all the time. Aware of their confusion, I decided without really knowing what this implied, to follow them wherever they would go.

even if burning

They are the only ones who say this. You and I can agree that the notion is absurd. It is not a logical error, or someone else's belief. It is a war.

dearest

The past changes

The ensuing conversation was far from being a pleasantly pastoral one. The old inherited fear. Rural magic and magic in the town. Psychoeconomics. They all volunteered. Satan fainted beneath the artillery.

make things mean

Their motto was the refrain. I want to believe you but you know how to lie. Mary Read was a pirate. We cannot breathe. You and I. We suffocate while we speak. It is the same time it was.

Sinbad paints horizons at the top of his pages. The real time of a life. Never. Plays against the music in his head. Eruption with clouds arranged by color. My hands are clasped behind my neck. I am in the ocean.

The assent. You agree to everything. You start the slow climb back to the entrance, past large drifts of Ginger Lilies and a magnificent bank of "Two Day Pink" Hibiscus. Travellers Palms on both sides a Jerusalem Thorn. Angel Trumpets hang straight down. From this point on you will see Plumbago, Inexorable, Sugar Cane, Chocolate, Begonias, Flamboyant, Tobacco and Gardenias. And near the end, Dwarf Bougainvillaea.

They are building a palace across the street. In the form of a letter. We are stuck in a storm.

# Spicer's City

When like palms with life

lines crossed as if memory

also didn't last

         you along the street seen

         dripping with trees

         the mind bright

We talked so long it burned my back. We never talk. My throat is bare.
The sun. Never there. Day or night.

or white but not

like this stone ball

or like this record

round

The world in your town drenched as they say. Speaking about your
absence. There is a register. A blur. A child tearing through the street.
Not like you either.

         high afternoon haze

         your day to be home

         In your day

is language strangely. You ask yourself what it would take. That taken. In the same words. A boy feels along the walls as if he were blind.

they take him

they taste him

angrily

The street is torn apart. The old street hidden and changed and hidden again. The new material. We don't sing. Our steps thrown back. The pavement as white as the sky. Hell with the women these flyboys.

but you are no pilot

we sit in Gino & Carlo's

at midday

The livid tables green as the child I mean when I say "We are not alone here." The music is identical. The pipes moan. There is less water than before. There is no rain at all

like real rain

I have not forgotten

we sound

the same when we say the same things like people of a certain time. As if history were not over. This is about the neighborhood of objects we are in. Someone is here. Is not here. It can be written the same way. It can't be said.

Black fish in paper bins. Water as clear as the sea. A boy playing hide and seek. A small boy. A large ceramic tree. He seems lost without you. He feels nothing.

yet as time

pretending to be

you or I

Frankly I have come here for you. Some things are brutal. There will continue to be works about gardens but this isn't one of them. This is the real world. Or is this the world? Do I have time for a quick one before whatever passes for night around here passes?

distant bit of roof

pink and red pales

wall of gold

Chinatown finds itself open. All this silk. The old patterns imagined again burning. Torn or thrown away. Acres of it. Children dancing crazily to bells. No one tells them.

moon of iron

rock garden steps

am tired boy

oak and palms tried

Like criminals we

know too much. A deserted watering hold in the deserted West. The Polk Gulch. The Mediterranean sun divides its victims. Each searches for the other one. And I can still feel the burn. The new set of words. Obvious in its disguises. I have pictures of the empty room.

unconscious quotation

broken like bones

they were yours

Gay bones. Jay De Feo eyes. On both sides of you naked. Your face. Capable of anything. The accident of putting two things together. Any two. Any time. It's territory day in the islands. Also your fault.

gone all out

prediction

A man takes his breath in and I decide to get it back out again.

love of

Oh! Poor girl!

The scale is the same. The space between house and ancient building choked with greenery. The moist air between us. The con men play with each other. A hero is trapped in a pinball machine.

Poor taste

is never enough. My fever shakes this picture of trees. Blooming. Not everything that doesn't exist is me. I have nothing to explain. That seems shallow but goes in. Contains blood. Is round. The steaming tar like lava makes the new town.

the figure with strings

strung

A mannequin in a window manipulates a doll. Caught in the act of
being motionless. Her head turned away. Inasmuch as it is a head.
He seems to fly. His arms held out. They are arms. Our arms. It
follows with the logic of a false similitude left from another age. We
believed in that too. Christ what innocents. Whose will go first?

Like firecrackers in the Broadway Tunnel. The continuous roar
between things. He claims not to understand negative space. The soft
skin. The mute discipline no one is ready for. We say nothing to each
other. Day after day. The celebration is ruthless. There is a musical
version of the past.

> caught in the radio

> is constant danger

> Also I am

constant also caught. The indecipherable note pasted like a rose to
the wall barely lit by the sun going down. Is clear to someone. Or
like a castle under siege. Overgrown with Edenic trees. The worse
for the wind raging above this solidity. Things made of stone subject
only to the catastrophes we know don't change things. Or change
completely but we remain unshaken. We are the objects. The people
were destroyed. More than once.

> we were just words

> like the pear is a fruit

> and is yours

and is filled with sun like the valley with the white roses pictured here. You can almost see the heat. The petals blurred as if unsure of themselves. The rain also pictured.

rains

naked from the waist

smokes or steams

Because the heat is relentless. It never rains when it's hot here. Petals for eyes. Something new pasted over the new thing. A child holds you to its lips. A highrise where the hotel. Also of granite.

A burned out pit. Graffitied man alive at the bottom with what did you expect written in red paint. A tent made of paper. The moon is still empty. But it will never be like it was. Known to not exist. The new moon.

is midday

We lay down in the lightest possible sun. She sang while it was too hot to move. But now it's not. Kuan-yin ice white Chinese goddess of love. Old red flowers turning yellow. Things disappear in the fog. He referred to certain people as the neighborhood.

still here

we are gone

This is the series of stone steps that don't go on. The animals squirming.

# From *Symmetry*

# The Muse

The familiar paraphernalia

Forced into the role of silent collaborator

The psyche at stake

We are in business together

The buildings melt into the sky

You sing to distract me

Your reason is not mine

Is mine

# That explode together

It gets worse   It gets better
The words seem to shrink
He writes about his experience
I write about mine
Song lyrics on her lips
Make the same sound
The automatic movements were the ones
Isolated like notes
I tell everything in plain words
Thinking against the action
The body changes what is said
I also write in zeroes
The flexibility is exact
He reads as if the words were his
He treats the book like an accordion
She belongs to El Diablo he sings
Over and over they agree
He tears it apart a capella
Her nerves are numbered like stars
Too distant to record

# Elaboration

stag

pant        flute        stoop        tent

flower     string      flag        slat

cup         lip                     fist

last                                 stem

rain        rest        red         sift

soft

# The missile

The protected zone
Like a diagram of a pinecone
Removed from life
Lightning
Seems alive

The quiet voice
The trees of an imaginary paradise
Dropping down

Or not fallen
Like people who are innocent
To the ground

To the air or back down
What lasts is what we have

What we have done

You pull me

To you I am

What can be

Unsaid

In a speech

What can this be

That sounds

Hard before

You pull me

Think you say

Nothing later

Or something shaped

So that it changes

The same way

You pull me

# The Procuress

If you cause me to act
By your most intimate will
You put your hand on the breast
Of the procuress red
As if through a lens
Sharpens the senses
The subject in relief
Handmade lace gold coin thick
Glass again see through completely
Is this account without meaning
To remain you turn back
To look over your shoulder at nothing
Or at darkness pictured
The places covered with linen
Again we begin
If you cause me
To act on your behalf
A verbal contract in other words
Not valid but accurate
A feminine form imagined
To consist of penstrokes instead
Of flesh we speak of her
In the third person
As if there were a difference
Between us the obvious one
Of being what we are
Not able to see
That this is all it is
Statement and persuasion
An analysis of the physical aspects
Of sight speaking candidly
The desirable things

Their antitheses
Love itself embodied perspective
Flattened out into a map
If you cause me to act

# What is said

Their words can be used against them

They are faithful and confident

We are them in their sense

In ours we dance to a slow song

One example of a solution is strength

Or in numbers

Where we are multiple

The story is said to unfold

Their words to be said again

By others pretending to be us

But they are men/women and we are women/men

It's like another planet

Or like people who don't see themselves

Though they stand before each other

Their words said

What is claimed

A companion piece to what is said\

If I had to put it all on red

Or on black I would be a gambler

And this would be my story

But I am not that

Object if you will or if not

This is not a practice hand

What is claimed

Is that chance exists

Spinning us in or out

Time is on the side it's always on

Like a bracelet like the physical

Hand it surrounds

What is claimed

# No closure

The window breaks down
Stunned and surrounded
There is no horizon
Where I am
Not less

Breath not breath
Stay
With no reason
Than here

It begins it began
The same "projecting
the transient closure of a casual gaze

into a concentrated field
of divine fixation."

But what is an image?

# There is no

Lack of harmony

Between form and meaning

Symmetry

# Plumas

Flashing jay. Stellar. Wings and body. Sky. Lake. Blue vase. Ultra. Deep night. Stratosphere. Ink.

The roof pale blue. The trees black.

Cloudy though still warm.

A discordant chorus.

Fowl.

Chimera. A fox. Stunned by light.

At dusk a man fishes for trout.

Lamplight. Kimono. Night again.

Day again. Goose quill.

We write.

Down and feathers. Inland beach. We read.

About symmetry about

Sound.

Spoon against cup. Toast.

Surface choppy. Husband. Thought.

People sleep in rented boats.

Geese on the beach. Grass and clover.

There is a storm. The lake is audible. The rain sweeps from the west. Our boat seems.

The memory of something. The waves were gold. I dream I know someone. But there is no point in knowing.

Reading about the city in the country. At night.

The air is filled with the sound of a piper.

Writing.

The city of those thinking about the city.

Up here they are a deep.

Afternoon sleeping. Blue.

The cell receives information in material form.

Time of day. Storm.

Coffee. Notebook.

"The very concept of a form, with an internal self-'reflection' or duplicate of itself as its defining characteristic—the concept, in other words, of symmetry with its constitutive dualisms (reflectional symmetry and rotational symmetry, asymmetry as itself determined by symmetry and so on)—implies a circumscribed space: a body with contours and boundaries."

A book with a sky on it. *The Production of Space.* Lefebvre.

Or song.

"The casket is empty
Abandon ye all hope
They ran off with the money
And left us with the rope."

The Pogues.

The blue dishes we bring from home.

Goose. Geese.

Leaves among them. A small one with a loud song.

Osprey.

Sleep before diving.

We sleep or walk.

Thick with flowers.

The blue dock.

When we move
The objects have a new arrangement
But are the thoughts
We recognize in them
What "we"
"And as for me" (from a song)
As as for me
Not knowing

Summer seems dark though the days are long. The brightness is flooded
with an absence of memory and obsession. There are questions.

Unasked. We get ready to go but don't go.

Questions about possibility.

A single and occasional cloud of butterflies in the heat of the day. Goose down.

Noon and wind.

What we are
When most (unconsciously)
The same is a remembered
Song from a movie of a book
About memory A part
Altered to fit the music
When we play (ourselves)

*Cabaret*

I have you then.

A jar of wings.

Two clowns in a canoe.

A blackbird shaking the bright body. Black and blue. Yellow.

Left shaking. Wings.

Black and white lake. Night.

My sleeping. Rented.

Seen from a chair in the corner.

Love.

Bucks Lake, Plumas County, May, 1992

# Diagram

"Practice is Art   If you leave off you are lost"
                        —William Blake

For discovery at a future time
A wooden something
Spent the morning writing letters
A spinning air

The western dragon
Weather written on its back it
Is the sky falling
Horned and whiskered

Blake's Laocoön
Waking whispered to me
"I dreamed I was writing …"
"Practice is …"

Raising his arms in the air
He says everything
Seeing the head through the hair
The printed veins

Paper is an active background
Both of us inside
This preoccupied creature
Painted

To look like good luck
Or like blood
Stays inside or doesn't
This animal

Is a pattern
Legible from above
Looking down at a body
Not in pain

The twister took the walls
Grandmother and child
Anymore
But would rather be

Today in paradise
Can be read from either side
The body doesn't fall away
Or does fall

Into a certain shape
You smile or read in your sleep
You wake up in it
Or partly wake

A common thing
Like breathing
But more ornate
As food also

Stays inside or doesn't stay
Sleeping after the game
Sleeping before the game
A city as if through the air

Repeatedly falls
Asleep during the emergency
The rumpled surface of a person
Quiet now

The grandmother might have said
But the child would have known
There is no such animal
Everywhere

The tail in your hair
And mouth and eyes
Bursts out the walls
People die

Unquietly
Sitting anyway
A creature eats   A saint
Emerges hands folded against

A metallic rhythm
Painted on a book
Patroness of how things hold together
And are torn

Face to face with a dragon
Actually a puppet inside
A man inside loose clothing
Wet

For some terrible reason
An exact replica
Of a thing that can't be known
Some mindless storm

Already past
Or went on forever
Only the visibility changing
Or the negotiations

There were no negotiations
You leave or you don't
You can't argue with the weather
The breathing of this animal

In not compatible with breath
Unless the air of the world
The very thing we want
To include in not included

Which changes the creature
Inside and outside
The sense of the storm, breathing,
Negotiation, death and representing

Impossible as I stand
Or sit waiting for another
Sound to come out recognizable
As life

There is always time
For the whole storm
Is made up like the animal
Startled

Rain late in the season
To do things
Staying inside all of one part
Of one day going on

From *The Case*

# Ghost Atlas

1.

"Lakes are the most ephemeral surface features of the earth…"

George and Bliss Hinkle, *Sierra Nevada Lakes*.

Working in the debris of rockets

We take pictures. We picture ourselves among rockets. White and initialed. Symmetrical. Rockets miss. More are sent. This morning though it's not war.

Launched.

*Blessed Assurance.* She writes about Amarillo. The final assembly point. She decides to stay. Citizen of the millennium.

The death of Smithson. The same physics.

Low to the ground. Cataclysm. Quiet.

Theory. But everything in what sense?

They always hit something.

What constitutes a town?

Not a natural lake except in that it was inevitable. Milky with debris.

Cyanide. No swimming.

The abandoned trailer edged in pink like a valentine.

Inscribed or transcribed.

Algae red salt in warm solution. Wading through this viscous medium on basalt rocks placed so as to demand attention. Grabbing hold of sharp crystals. Doubtful support. In a context of going. Going out into a finite sea.

A waltz called "Tales from the Farside" fills the car and now the room and then breaks down.

Nick dreams the oil refinery in the backyard is on fire and firemen are stealing the rosé.

Telemetry. Bill Frisell does a plucking thing at the end of the next piece. Hearing it in the car eyes watering.

Mud crystal salt grid from memory.

Sitting by an open door in September.

The library in our garage dark from the outside.

Two sources of order.

Life organizes itself in mud then dies. Things die at different rates.

Both people I saw that movie with are dead.

*Dangerous Liaisons*

Identifying with John Malkovich even when he plays the maniac.

Disproportionate response.

It's nice to have a friend.

2.

The destroyed place is beautiful.

Dead letter. Dead end. A writer does a search for dead and includes the links in his homepage. A writer edits an issue of his magazine around death. A man holds a gun to his head and makes him drive his cab around the city. He doesn't die.

Golconda, NV 89414

"Et en Utah ego"

I learned that line as a child in my first art event.

Poussin. Later we lived in the house in the painting. I could see that movie a thousand times.

John Coplans, *Robert Smithson's Sculpture*, "The Amarillo Ramp":

"Once you are on the bluff again, you are reminded that even if you think you know the pattern of the world, you still have to move through it to experience life."


3.

The yellow walls of Café Gitane.

In New York he reaches for his cup.

His politics. The disease in each of us.

Later in California a camellia is forced open by the autumn heat.

Dark yellow cash register, red upholstery.

An old woman in the sun across the street.

Her expression. His face.

Muñoz figures weighted down by their connection to the world, to each other.

Walls coated with H. P. Lovecraft grey. *The Colour Out of Space*.

She has brought her own chair.

Fear of reading that story.

"they lacked the power to get away"

We go see Muñoz sculptures at the D I A. Jerry had wanted to use a photo of Muñoz for the cover of *Rome, A Mobile Home*. After his death I search for the image. I am unable to locate the artist or make an agreement with his gallery. Nick finds a picture of another piece by Muñoz called "Waiting for Jerry" in a *Parkett* magazine in the D I A bookstore.

A lighted mouse hole.

The tunnel mouth.

That image in *La Jetée* following the line.

The survivors settled underground.


4.

Tango all afternoon of obsessive anxiety and passion.
Parrots (loud) and rats (they say) in the palm trees on Dolores.
Lorca's waltzes translated and retranslated.

The Macondo café.

Pink silk satin shirt
Soaked with sweat nearly
Blinding walk from China Basin
Or walking in anger apart

Away why doesn't she just walk

Away in the distance pictured
Inexact not even a memory
She takes on the madnesses
And is driven (though she drives) by them

The rules of a made place
More than the world pulls her
(She wants this) down leaves
And returns and she is an athlete

Of returns she practices the nuance
Of the accepted step and turn
And step the measure of which
He pretends to think is natural

That nature is this dance
But she is movement only there is
No difference between this and the threat
Never not present

And then finally not and completely
(The thing feared) forgotten.
Again other lovers encountered at night
One makes the other in a book into Christ

(With revenge) like too many notes
Bent backwards or transfixed
Or calls—a sense of falling
The controlled dangers we plan

We watch her die and want to smoke
We like knives
The room is huge and soiled and white
Sordid, gilded, holds us up

Like steel rods in her painting
Volcano or womb he says He
Doesn't say cunt He doesn't say
(She signs her name) what disappears

What he wants (everything)
For the fake world to be real
Or nothing which abruptly
The song starts up, draws him in


5.


A condition exacerbated by music
We are not the faces of the future
In that movie. We lack both
The power supply and the mobility
Through time that Chris Marker pictured
In the pure modernity of the sixties
Unlike now a blur of times with no

Future pictured in the remake
Beyond the dark city which
Is an italic present like the cigarettes
In *Blade Runner* or the song in *Brazil*

I search for *Idoru* and find a virtual
Lascaux designed by a guy I met
Obsessed with the Neolithic who wanted
Only to talk ten thousand years of agriculture in cafés
His prize possession a letter
Allowing him to scan caves
(Apparently he did what he wanted)
We want the story of that darkness.
He carried it with him. He said
All I need is a little time


6.


Home because migraine
Brain too cold or too large for head
Generations of poets marching through
Whalen/McClure birthday event
Keith Abbott saying Et en Arcadia etc.
David Meltzer that time marches
All over one and looking somewhat trampled
Another widow among the readers
Himself but reads most
Musically of anyone

Ghosts off the scale that day
Disembodied voices facing
The wrong way into time

"It won't help you. It won't help others.
It won't change anything."

Leslie's frog erotics
Ditto Bob's sacramental distribution of the cake
(A thousand years of catering in every gesture)
Alice Notley predicts her own silence

Kit gets the laughs
"People see me; they like that
I try to warn them it's really me."
Kevin Killian brings Eddie Berrigan like a child bride
Norman reads a *Diamond Noodle* counting poem
Is stunned to know you

Whalen unwilling love god
Sits like a scepter
Stands in slow motion
Blowing out candles which don't
Stay blown
No one objects to his perfection


7.


*The White Rose*
"She calls him her ghost"

Norma Cole and Phoebe Gloeckner are in a movie, actually Kevin
Killian's play *Wet Paint*, but let's say a movie of the life of Jay DeFeo.
They are artists. They are twins. They have dangerous beauty.
Disaffected. Smoky and disenchanted. Still. In the movie they have
their say. Full face but quiet. They play it for effect, consciously and
unconsciously, for sex. Most erotic when most withheld. They refuse
the center of attention, standing just off where you think you can go,
making the center empty.

The score is sad
Artist odalisque on her painting in its box

But clothed the film rough
Film to video transfer decays

Can you lie on your own painting
In someone else's movie?

Will you be covered with paint
Will the situation be yours

To exploit at will but what
If there's nothing you want?


8.


"On the tenth day images
Begin to appear like confessions"


The return alters time
Irrevocably the loop or detour


This is  now because construction
Is incessant nothing normal even


The route not the route we know
How can this be real time?


The order is fucked into eternity
The movie is made only of pictures


I watch *La Jetée* several times on tape before I remember that I have
also made a movie of stills. Jiri Veskrna and I made a five minute video
"Before the War" in 1989. We were not thinking of Chris Marker's film.
We were thinking about war and technology. We were in love with

fear. Any time might be defined as "before the war." We simply figured there would be another one. The tendency of trauma to obliterate time and memory was less of an interest for me then. When I saw *La Jetée* as a student, my film teacher was obsessed with the woman's face at the end of the movie and with one painted by Vermeer. He felt they were the same. There was nothing I could do with the knowledge that this woman was myself. And later when I was the face of death I knew something I had hoped not to know. There was a quiet in it I didn't want. Being awake and asleep. The dream where you can't run. The wrong two things.


The jetties aren't based on each other
The words are the same


But only those two
There's no jetty in the second movie


*12 Monkeys*
A red spiral


Neither collaborator saw the first movie
Some of the people involved die


The number of movies gets infinite
We have breakfast with Abby Child at Café Gitane


"I am forgetting" she writes
(In *Motive for Mayhem*) presumably sometime

Before I write the same line
She puts a thousand movies together


Watching our tape
I am surprised to find movement in the stills


They have the saturated color of paintings
Not a movie but distancing


A presentiment careless of the future
"Moments like these are just like other moments"


"This sophism was accepted as destiny in disguise"
(broken statue) "the man whose story this is"


9.

And so we go back
Having felt but not seen

The thing we came to see
Squinting out into the pink

Inland ocean remnant
Of what we want

Salt peaks
History of salt

The Museum of Tobacco and Salt

The accidental reading of the future
That we were there

Kid science fiction
Rocket man, arms crossed on chest

Like pharoahs these monuments
We need hardly repeat

It was stabilized collusion
The unreported fire

From *Nude Memoir*

1.


The nude is given
The nude is not a woman

Who displays a tendency to be naked

An artist keeps the whole game in mind

From her he learns
Replaced by physical presence

"With eyes shut like a bride…"

Taken she says of the pictures
Red of the lines

Directions for building the nest in which the nude is to lie are preserved
in a notebook. A facsimile. Silence is maintained by the artist.
Madeleine or Mary. She has a long view to a wall of windows. A writer
remembers his mother who is dead. The red is self-explanatory. She
was friendly with the wrong man. An artist. A con artist. Later a cast is
made and something like skin is stretched, they say, with tenderness.
The wall of the world outside the window includes a tower like the
one in the movie. They move through the city as if they were alone in
it. *Vertigo*.

I'm telling a story
That didn't happen
She claims  He is angry


Red X Two red X's
A notebook of facts
The first thing to fall

The sky is reflective
And transparent her story
Likewise she says

He writes in remembered paternal speech. In resistance to her. She
is in trouble with time. The pattern of their lives together. There is a
contraption but not in the picture. Some people see her as dead, but
not her face. It can't be seen. Jean. Her eyes can be seen through the
mask which is untitled. Her child stares back at her. Diana the hunter.
The queen.

Added numbers                                    Blankly
Ink or water                                     Notes

                        Quiet now

At that time                                     Baby
But why?                                         But not

Alive. The lamp seems alive. It took a long time. All of life to get to the
end. There are letters and photos reproduced here. In the movie she is
saved over and over. She (I) was overcome when she saw the display.
It was a relief to see it. Like being dead again. It was a monument to
sex. Of her sex. A series of enclosures with a name but no explanation.
A statue or statute. A reign.

Felony                                           Statutory
Proviso                                          Bent

                        Murder

Miscreant                                        Informant
Citizen                                          Provocateur

When we kill the doe we call it venison. We kill each other. The body is a corpse. A corpus. (A work.) There is a Latinizing as the stiffness sets in. There is a figuring out but only in retrospect. He learns her death. Her terms. He learns the movement in the tomb with diagrams. It's not a house but a necropolis. There is land and water and flowing hair. She is disheveled.

Shovel
Spat
Squirm
Squat
Bitter
Stem
Seam
Twist
Bitten

2.

She is Judy now. The words accumulate with the quality of being mere. A permanent reversal of time occurs. With oneself as the vanishing point the lines regress. The whole thing is built on a floor made of squares, but you can't see it.

A woman fills the frame. There is terror. Her costume is evidence. Still life. Mediation. Immediate. She decides to go with it. She is a real woman. Her decisions have terrible consequences. It is difficult to say. It is impossible to know. Or not to know. No one is guilty. No one is left.

A writer writes with numbers. Marcel. With pictures. His thought balloons resemble her thinking. He laughs because he knows. Eddie. Edward. He punctuates the situation with laughter. But too much has happened. Jimmie. She is still ticking backwards but can't think. Her name is Kim. She was named for the war.

Preoccupation
Her occupation is delay

The ricochet of looking

Several meetings later

The edges of the photo and paragraph

Like parentheses, a board game or his arms

"His eyes," she began

"Abrazos," he wrote. Akimbo

"Writing this to you...." She began to investigate and fix the attentions around her, but the picture was mute. Her arm is the pattern of one, her sex of another. Leather stretched over a metal armature. The problem has features of interest. He is a master detective. He is a petty thief. A petit bourgeois. A middleman. "A world in yellow" Because light. "...heart feeding telephorically..."

The spidery writing of the notes in *The Box of 1914*. Marcel Duchamp, American, 1887-1968. He was not afraid to be naked. She had known him for a long time—or not. It was never clear. There was no similarity between his passion and that crime. But there was a continuum. People turn away from the image of death. Nothing was left of his thinking but these objects. This century and counting. Grim whimsy.

Diana puts together suspension systems beginning at 5 a.m. Energy. Apollo. The male nude. The female worker. Automobile. Moves and comes to rest. Potential movement. The machine. "Eyes shut like a bride…" (Adorno) Stumbling into position. Precision. Accountability. Exhaustion is the steel in her eyes. She is a real woman. Paradise.

"another fetid nest" (Wieners)

Address

And expelled again

They knew they were naked

His slim belly the slant

Of his eyes and wide

Shoulders unzipped

Fly but an action

The unzipping (Wieners again)


3.


His work was language. There was nothing about. He spoke. He smoked. There was a metamorphosis of his body into air. Single room. Hotel. Implication. Visitor. A woman traveled with him. Later her story emerged detail by detail. He implied. They were the same person. The mythology was too old to be written. "She died," he thought, "for this?"

A speaking likeness

The description

Unbearable speech

Document

Made of words her

Eyes and mouth missing

Or reassembled

The desecration

The gangster vivid

Madeleine pictures her own eye. A spiral. There is a turning inside. Inside out. Hers is an active surface. She lies on her stomach. She lies on her back. Moisture in the room. In her mouth. *Semina*. In her mind a collection of pictures and verses. *Versus*. He was in them. In person. The picture takes him in. She has made herself into that woman. She has included details. Anatomically impossible features. She looks dreamy trying to remember the words. "Every word is born of a sex offered to a face." (*The Duchamp Effect*)

She renders herself. Kim. Creatural sadness. But it was not life that interested him. "Ovaire toute la nuit" The horns of a bull pressed against her, head at crotch level. Skeleton. Ex goddess. She is thrown from the tower because of her knowledge of life and death. Her complicity in the incident is at the heart of the madness of the hero. He depends. She bends over backward for him. For them. Her falling body is like a rag doll.

152

Her work was language. *Vertigo*. He doesn't believe in the artist who paints herself unless it is her flesh she paints. But his belief is irrelevant. Diana is not a writer. She is a hunter. Punctuation but no words. Lines that are portraits. Automobile. Her mobility. That day she was pictured in his car. That night. The huntress hunted. Her hair almost white in the moon. The sun.

Age of gold
A child with the memories of a woman

A boy a son
A court

The mission

Laid out like a garden
The window is black

A courtyard
He *sees* the wound

Around her neck. The fatal necklace. "You shouldn't save mementos of a murder." Desperate at this point but only because of the sound. Hypnotic queen of the forest stuff. Soft spoken. She was found in the car. She was found in the tall grass.

Typographical
Error
Car
Left in the lot

The all night
Sorry
Spent
Details of the

Dawn

The grass wet and wakes not thinking of death. Innocent on one side and on the other not. Of the fact of it. The twenty-second. Twenty-third? psalm. "Though I walk…" Palm, like an oasis of death. From death. "A stiff hand held out." The arms stretched up. Flung. The burial place was there. That action. The solstice was the hinge of the door. The threshold is an attractor. We go back down.

4.


We visit the grass. Ordinary grass on a typical day. We open ourselves expectantly staring at the hill. The slope is familiar and meaningless. We are pictured there. We see the pictures and spend the money but the image remains.

Orchids dyed blue. Stained. Dahlias. A flower like a carnival. Blue. Betty. A black mass. He keeps a record of his progress. He doesn't expect to come back. She is also not expecting. In fact she is bleeding. She never reaches the change. She remains unchanged. His book is a memoir. An action. Red.

Read the book before dying
*The Black Dahlia*
Counting the pages before your death
Like any Scheherazade

A quiet night with a book

Ellroy by Estrin read
Fell asleep (woke dead)
Later I (who?)
Claiming there are no

Coincidences which are not language. Therefore legible in the old sense. Not sense as in naming but as in the five senses or directions. "'the 5 perfections and the 5 hindrances'" (Wieners) The longing which connects us. The arrangement of meanings. The late night interrogations. Memory like cash wildly spent. Holed up alone. Marcel in his hotel in Munich. He invents a woman. Indestructible. Incomplete. Compartmentalized. She descends.

Body/stiff
Kiss/smack

Sip/suck
Steam/ream
Touch/slap
Fuck/stuff
Buss/bang
Fought off
Succumb

"Let your mind go and your body will…" But what will it do? The spinning woman in our minds. A common. Wretch. Wench. Assembly required. He paints a red X here and an arrow there, over the next. The photos are dark. Evidence assembled before the crime. It isn't a crime to die. The body doesn't follow. He is pictured with a woman whose body curves around itself like a medieval letter. Cranach. He is a model Adam. His insinuating hand

Cupped
The stoppages

Villainy
The string stretched

Or wound
Pronounced dead

Dressed up
Disclosed

Disposed of

Unceremoniously. Someone else takes care of it. La maja fracasada. Takes it away. Furniture put in the street. A stranger takes it away. A red table from our life together replaced by the glass table of my life alone. Diana also buys a glass table. A glass house. To see and be seen. Not. To be known.

Things arranged on the table. Typewriter. Orchid. Glass laced with metal. Papers. A box with a book in it. *Rollywhollyover*. John Cage plays chess with Duchamp. Duchamp with a woman in another book. Her breasts, she remembers, swollen with hormones. He is focused on the game. She is naked (nameless). We don't recognize her.

5.

She works naked. It is hot that summer. Windows open. Shades drawn. Paper. Ink on hands then mouth. One room life. Nude sitting. Nude on the bed. In the chair. Nude with glasses and pen.

Hunger at night

Heat dawn sequence

Too quiet to eat

Too hot to breathe

Stoppages pictured

A ligature stretched

A metric

To eat, breathe and stop in time

To repeat

The illusion is the sense of change. Being transient. Barely occupying a place. The change changes again. The letters are translucent. In the box are personal letters reproduced on translucent paper. It's called a circus (again the spinning woman) but is more like a museum, a mausoleum.

There is a translucent monument drawn by Erik Satie of a tower like a wedding cake. A *Castle*. "Courtesy Archive de la Foundation Erik Satie" And other drawings of smoke. Musical realism. The life of sounds. Her throat. There was a circus which traveled. The wheel was the wheel of fortune. A chance novel one reads.

Through the glass you see a window, a courtyard and a fountain. You see *The Given* through a crack, a hole unlike a window. It is, of course, a peep show. The show is a contraption. A scaffolding of leather to seem like flesh. "White" flesh. A mental frame. Hairless. Unveiled. Given but hidden. Supine but not at rest. Never at rest. Exposed. *Given*. Donnée. Dona. Our lady of extremities.

Represents flesh here
Viewed or for penetration or
Eaten but consummately
Available but fake but realistic —
Symbolic but complicated (dese-
crated) Slaves traveled naked
The history of flesh forthrightly
Exposed during an exchange. Choice
As in delectable not as in choosing

not to go. We believed we would be eaten and wanted not to go. (Equiano's narrative) Spoke. The wheel again. The vicissitudes of living in a world where you don't officially exist. People like you. The model for that cunt belonged to the slave-owning class. There is a continuum. But the arm came from his wife. The lamp she holds. Liberty. Liberté.

A blueprint. The white taken from the flag. (Haiti) Slave owners feared the idea of revolution for obvious reasons. The dream of killing generated by the killed person. The rendered person. Torn or drawn. Split. Returned. Rend: "To lacerate (the heart, soul, etc.) With painful feelings" (*OED*). Render: "The act of rendering an account, statement; account of expenses." A notebook with meticulous entries. Reduced to writing. But reassembled. Death being but one of the differences. The list of Oulipo includes all the members alive or dead. Render. "To play or perform." Member. To belong, to be assembled with. "Remember me."

To give in

To give in return

To return

Rent
Encounter
Reconnoiter

Arrive at

Land (encompass)

See


6.


You can see yourself in the box. In the museum you look back at yourself. The object is present but encased in a force field of reflection. The white walls of the museum and the organized space of the poem. Exquisite context. Corpse of course but legible. Beautiful death. *Die in order not to die.* (Lyotard) Civic death, not the burned toe-tag of your loved one. An aesthetics of dust and history. Rags arranged. Which is the real dust?

158

The web site as box. Dustless realm. Media. *In media*...Immediate rest. She thought she was somewhere when she was there. Wrote code, searched. Prevaricated. Tabled. Scanned herself. Young and then old. *In media vita.* She writes with her hands but she can render in any form. Any format. The naked problem in a new form.

Nudity is common there. A key word. All the words are used. A few lines constitute a figure. The fewer the better. Various responses make us believe our interlocutor is sentient. What creates belief? A key word is made into a question. The question into a challenge or objection and so on. We find satisfaction at the lack of personal qualities in this strategy. It is the method itself we wish to engage.

Bullet
Bulletin

Beast
Breast

Life
Lite

Gist
Jest

Gesture

*In Motion Speaking.* What the nude doesn't do. The sum of this shattering. (The body supine on the bed.) Notes made on the nude in the margin of the book *The Nude* in relation to the naming (we did this) of that section (Nudes) of *Rome, A Mobile Home. A Funny Thing Happened on the Way to the Forum.* Buster Keaton sets out on a long journey. His eyes dazed. Old Stoneface.

Two nudes in bed editing. They argue about lines. Agree to a version. Words. The word statue is proposed, but is too eyeless. There is a visceral quality to nudes. She puts her hand on him in a healing gesture. His torso twists away though he turns to her. Face. As if holding onto the world. The version exists but he might have changed it. Pre/version. The perverse finality of.

"White hills canceled by color / Inward cakes of creamy nothing / Ramshackle rush-hour and yourself a souvenir" Estrin in stone on Van Ness and Market. Now almost worn away. Familiar. Days of driving. Of rain. When I walked everywhere in the city. Relentless walking for miles. Took cabs. Jerry drove. I never drove. Occasionally I rode in his cab. He came to my restaurant. He pretended to be a driver. Me a waitress. It was the uniform. It was realism. There were foreigners. We gave our names. Rudy and Naomi.

I don't speak
About it This
Isn't me you see

Before you I
Singular or the plural
I (we)

You and me
Objects now
Spoken for

But arbitrary. The high restaurant window. He hired me on the spot. I put on an apron and went to work. It was a sex thing but I didn't have to put out. An imaginary nakedness. Earlier job at a naked place. The Bijou. Thirteen hour shift. Two days. Sent me to the drugstore to put on makeup. I sold tickets. Sent me there for pain killer. The street car. Up and down Market. The old men at the ticket counter.

7.

The aura preceding the headache wasn't visual. It was a shimmering in the perception, as if to perceive the pulse of the world inappropriately, loudly. To know too much. Congestion like the street. A rushing sound. Water. The stream through the heart. The flood. She called for him, they say, from the car.

An apparition in the forest. A woman in a thicket. Maja fresca. The swiftness in the original included as part of the incident. She spoke of a way of looking. "It's what I'm for." Of cashing in for the victims. A person in a system. A time card. Punching in and then out. Inexorable closure. The factory and the forest. The line. She disappears in a collision of lines.

Of lies

His work was to lie

And she naked in the pictures and

Thorns finally

Didn't lie

Or isn't alive so can't die

Only the ones left

Know anything

And they don't know

He thinks to make a logic out of it. Marcel or Ellroy. To achieve a pure dimensionality he travels. He rents a room. Thinks with his mind.

Of stopping. With pleasure. Measure includes elements of suspense. He remembers everything. He charts that retention. He is capable (culpable) of mere speech. He calculates the future, but feels drawn down into time. He thinks with what is not his mind.

The trick takes the money

An offering is expected

Like a telegram or an accountant. He counts. He has the ability to persuade women with a series of figures, an allusion and a punch line. Into anything. A woman becomes anything. Amazing feat. Twist in midcentury, mid-air.

But she needs no persuasion. Madeleine. Magdeleine. Already naked as if bursting, smashing or tearing herself, her clothes, her surroundings. She got to it. She was ahead. A whore. A horror. An appalling availability dawned on him. A blow. His own torso emptied of air. Breathing slowly now. Heart not going. Then going too hard. Stops in the head. An epithet or act. Loud. She was too loud.

He made no statement. What happened was the only proof that he had existed. But what happened? In the new arrangement of old evidence there was no closure. He personified closure and wanted to kill it. Victim by proxy. She was a "being for others" in her last moments. Matter only.

"physical agent of love"
Or party girl you decide

She wore a lined bolero
Danced at the drop of a hat

Drank with a vengeance
Was self-sufficient in fact

Having a more filled-out
Existence than the men she

Liked them mean and sleazy she


8.


was disillusioned. Betrayed by old friends. Women and men. In ways
that she could not explain. But she knew. A child would have known.
Had she? Did they? The mixed tenses of the dead. She saw them. The
friends. Straight through to the wall and ground. Betrayal like death.
Transparent window or widow.

There is a court in which there is no redress. It is not a place. It is
the function of that space to keep anyone who enters from being able
to make her case. There is no case. The Code Noir was designed to
justify African slavery by seeming to regulate it. In it people are defined
as things, "beings for others." The Enlightenment intellection used
to perpetuate the Code cannot effectively end its influence. There
are too many points of complicity. The contraption that allows you to
speak by silencing me is not neutral or logical.

The crime can't be undone. There is no morally superior position in
relation to it. That morality is exactly betrayal. The court comes to
order each time a conversation occurs in which one interlocutor finds
herself to be above the situation. A person pretends to be a pillar but is
merely an erection. She regrets there is nothing she can do for you.

Victim that you are

You get yourself killed
He takes you seriously

He discovers that pain is transferable
No one can name his behavior
Least of all you

History is his alibi
Women his obsession

But you are not a woman to him

It (I) she said was not just some painted clit. I was aware of the
implications of my dimensionality. My dimensionality caused me to
forget you. To forget the crime, though I remembered the dead. The
assassin was part of the memory. It was me. The non-existent past was
easier to grasp than the non-existent present. And then it wasn't. There
was blood. It was bloody. (I) got large, raining down over everything.

Stained. Some of the clothes were kept in bags but most were simply
thrown away. Bagged and trucked to a dump. Donated. *Given*. The
job of dispersal. Like worms we labor to break things down. To get rid
of everything. She found herself on her knees scraping the rug off the
floor. Nothing could be saved. Nothing could be known.

Equiano gets old. They get old together, but not yet. He writes a
memoir of captivity in the language of the captors. To tell them. She
does this too. Their language subsumes like captivity. And like it, retains
a resistant passion which draws one into the narrative. The hunger for
the language that destroys life. That owns form. The contract. The
act. "I am imprisoned in your language," she says. It was a seduction
strategy, but of whom?

His work was a tomb

Serrano's flesh

Piss poor but golden

An infamous but plain

Clerical humility

And then not

Hot and then

The flesh red after fire

Blue before

Cold. Spent the night in the open. Dead. Coolness of stars up through the ceiling imagined alone in the same bed. Quiet. Broken by remembered speech. Spoken for. To account for. How to account for the present situation. Gradual change marked on the skin like a measuring cup. The skin (again) painted leather. The hand held open. The answer. She raised her hand and kept it up.

9.

Ten minus one

She counted but was

not believed. The syllables like a mantra. The answer. Counting in order to rid herself of numbers, of time. The increments of the present. The same count. A decimal minus one reminds one never to go over or to go back. Not a sequence but a repetition like a song. A petition like a question. Never again. Duchamp as a form of grief. A diary. A display of the invisible. Of visible decay. The mode here is eliminative. It is the only mouth she has left.

"Piece of Ass Lost." The necropolis pictured by a dead poet in Ellroy's *Clandestine*. Poet cop. The mouthpiece of fate. Exploitation as love. Women who don't get older. Women as men. It doesn't matter. The U.S. number one in violent death just past Mexico and Brazil. First in the First World and the Third. The guardian of infested spirit. Someone follows a woman. She is not a muse but a fate. She talks too much. They drink together. They eat. Is she one of many or a singular masterpiece. Impossible to follow him down that street. The action is complete to the degree that it is not legible. Or transferable to another medium. It is not unfinished but undone. Not the crime but the gun. The piece of string with which you hope to find yourself. Missing. She was missing in her head. What we have is a reconstruction.

Diana watches herself on TV. She wanders absently around the house. She is not dead. She is an artist. The interview reveals everything she hopes for. There is a queen and a corpse. She finds her cigarettes and begins to smoke. She is seventy. Voluptuous as parchment. Thickly written. She takes into herself a sense of death. She lets it out.

She wonders how to preserve access without giving in to a deadened sense of hierarchical exclusion. Now that authority has been shown to be the shuck it is. To provide a method for reading, to alter the activity of reading itself. In retrospect or in the sense that it has already taken place. She reads the scene before the crime. Or we wouldn't be having this conversation. His ambition is naked, mechanical. He also wants to read.

The vaginal scroll

She performs (Schneemann)

Memorably laid out

Source or origin

Like a physical note

Of itself sufficient

Opened like the book

She wrote

The reconstruction is sloppy. Bad. Not convincing. Not made to be so. Black velvet lines the unseen back of the door. To soften the blow. Her character pokes through her performance like bones through flesh. Judy. Judith. She loves him but he loves her double. Her twin. Who is convincing. A con, snare or fox. A pest. He likes the angularity. The bending back. But he falls during the kiss. He is injured. "I hate this," she says. He doesn't miss her then.

The scroll unwinding and the performer

Takes over removing

Her shroud her look

Distracted in the picture

She takes off

Her glasses her theatricality

Will be attacked in place of her person

He argues her down

Her desire is unknown

Impossible to predict its hold on him. "…a diagram of the cruel geometries of desire." The reviews are ambivalent. The scriptedness of their exchanges is painful to him. Her double jumps into the bay. The actor after. Also his double. Later on a sound stage wet close-ups. The real actors. His strained face dazed with obsession. The paleness of her hair, dark dress spread out but clinging also. Her limpness in his arms. He stares down at her, climbing imaginary steps out of the sea. Her high heels in silhouette. The twist of her waist is displayed to him, to us.

# From *Self-Destruction*

# Gone Again

Texture of stucco
Regarder of sounds (listener)
"reaching back in the night to grope for a pillow"
Finding you are not home
"not yet at the edge"
For it is *who* that appears and disappears
"You are also like this [but] who could not be you?"
When bombs fall
The disappearance is adorned
Momentum
Terror
Josephine
*My Disappearance*
The moon today
Not yet gone

# Convention

Not unlike the moon. Eyes open all the time. When we talk we sound the same for a while and then depart. We meet like conventioneers. I trade a definition of myself for a thousand years of history. Random House. Against the tempo. Back through the aisles unable to find where we are and then finding it. Finally the walls simply open and we walk out into the dusk. I had no idea what would happen. Even so I was wrong. We were wrong in our expectations.

# First Song

Tell me to sing
A series to serenade to calm
To clarify to drizzle
Walk go along to the ocean
Without light with light to the sea
You were with me in hell
It wasn't like hell
We were under the sea
The same as love you were/are
Tell me to embrace you
Carry you off two or three ways
How many in this song
How many times going
Gone by boat to the sea
More sacred to us than something
Tell me to hold you

# Place

This ache
Ageless
Longing
Age this

Place
Transit
Young age
Aching is

Age
Scene of our
Place our
Trance

This change
Transitive
Placeless
Age of

# Any Day

"Any year starts as a literal translation."
Alan Halsey, *Auto Dada Cafe*

Accoutrements of mind fully
Iron stairs the shaky stance

Of tenants identified as guests
Of themselves late at work still

I pay myself to be here
"Important things about to happen"

But which of these is it? The books
Cooked in this light the collected

Books arrive with your order
The maps include every detail

Brightness also hot and here
Dry but wet there

A paragraph per location biscuits
Promised every morning homemade

Jam but made there
In a state of constant replacement

She called. That was the echo.
Displacement in columns like numbers

Associated with gender but literal
I never get anywhere complaint

Translation project on-going
There were no exceptions to his love

# Josephine

Fine
Affinity

        Sign of

                      Seraphic
                      Phatic or
                      Fate

        Italic

                      Plant or
                      Gesture
                      Serene
                      Final

Pine

# Cryptophasia

Our language is not the only thing keeping us apart. The leaves are blinding in the morning. I didn't understand it to be physical but it was. We are. Information. Doubles. Our attachment to small talk means the world to me. He is telling his own story, making it up with chance input from the word and the world. He is a con artist. He is lost in his work. The leaves are white in the sun dating from before the war. Before either of us was born. But now we are born.

A woman sits in a room weaving a rug. It will be sold to support an organization for women. She could be killed for belonging to the organization or for weaving the rug. By chance there are two stories about this organization in the news. The phenomenon of there being two things—two of anything—has something to do with us. It's strange, the reasons there are to kill a person.

She is the character she is describing. The trick is to keep speaking in order to have responded to the interrogation. Small talk. There should always be two of something. She is the second of several things. The completion. The added on thing completes the initial entity, rounding out its possibilities—extending, even negating its potential. Finally, the entities become each other, are found to be the same or they switch positions. It's the only way we can tell we are not still in the war.

The businessman knows of the organization. Like the artist, he is in a high risk occupation. Like the women. Like us. He will say anything to the cops. He leaves clues to the falseness of his story, though in a certain way his story is precisely true. It proves that he will do whatever needs to be done, taking the situation to the next level a beat before the others in it have realized the inevitability of this step. Not like us with our small talk. Or exactly like us, like you.

Weakened by the moon

"Twin, me!" José Garcia Villa, *Aphorisms*

> Why now when you are no longer
> beautiful? (He said)
> She works for me
> Let her go
> Allegory of song

"Have you written anything in the past few weeks that has become newly meaningful to you?"

"Opposed to these two positions is the experience of the poet …"
Giorgio Agamben

> Apostasy
> Arrival intact
> Critique (She is with me)
> Semblance

"What Critics call the Fable is Vision Itself" William Blake, *Vision of the Last Judgment*

Capitalism continues

43 planets around other stars and counting

Their gravity weak like ours

Having arrived in heaven alone *Ambushed by God.* Instruments are being built to spy on the universe from the moon's heaven where it is always dark.

Distance marker

She is lost in the wilderness of her work. He is unable to perceive them as different from us. Sadly there is a difference. Trust turns out to have been an inappropriate response to the situation. A faulty belief system imposes itself on the physical laws. The results are the usual ones. We watch the unfolding. It's like a wave. We are folded in it. We rest there in our work. She and you and I. It is as if we are in love. He says we are in love with capitalism and that it will shatter all of my illusions. I say I don't have illusions. Which was true then.

He is lost in his work. He sinks into it. In that way we are indistinguishable. The disconnect is the moment we work toward. The accumulation is incidental. Right. He accepts the so-called physical laws but he is a stranger in the moral universe. He has me for that. That for me.

Is this the real world? I need to see a budget. This conversation is almost unnecessary. It is not a forgivable trespass. Not if it goes as planned. You pay for your beliefs. I pay for them also. It's a physical thing.

Moon of the planet of that star

Steel yourself

From Romanticism to the Avant-garde

> "Capitalism appears unannounced."
> Karl Polanyi, *The Great Trans-*
> *formation*

Against the day of the plunge into the unknown

Closely woven rows of knots—a garden that can be carried in the hand. He wants to give her the time in the form of money but she wants it in time. The knot in thought. The garden of a thousand years with its built-in perspective. Made to be carried off. To be sold.

180

House plus light plus sky

A transposition problem        "Two futures coincide"
                               Norma Cole, *Coleman Hawkins*
                               *Ornette Coleman*

The formal features of our relationship which has become in fact
entirely business begin to overwhelm its content. We are at the cutting
edge of the extremity of capital. Our designation is *Left Hand of
God*.

"We had willingly entered the time stream by an exercise of the free
mind ... no effort of the will power can ever lift us wholly clear of the
current." John Taine, *The Time Stream*

How comfortable are you judging the madness of others?

Blinding kiss

                               Anthem

Interspersed with             Chorus of
                              Please don't
                              Aria

Urgent at the table

Not a genuine "I" thought and yet convincing though we didn't know
we were ourselves at that point. She was able to help him with his
trouble. "What do I have," we said, "if I don't have you?"

He is lost in the wilderness of his work. He is not aimless but driven.
His being lost is not the source of the trouble. The trouble is the
philosophical isolation of the cascading series of panic attacks that
constitute his daily life. Light on the table in the afternoon. The leaves

again. A feast of light. "I'm sorry," we said, "to fuck with you in this way." We admit, "It will probably happen again."

There is a light in his eyes that says, "But why not go with them into this hungry death? Go straight on to the end."

"My body had been blasted clean out of space and time. Where I had existed there was a void." Taine.

A voice

The last individual in the species
                              Choir

His oration                   Acquire
                              Chant
                              Chance

The self of ecological optics

Not typical of stars


Until the wood begins to glow like the sun. I imagine being here alone and then realize I am alone. He is lost in the wilderness. But I in the music. Out behavior is criminalized. We say we are joined at the hip. That I am also lost. And the light spills over onto the floor.

"The monuments will reveal what truth there is." Eric Temple Bell, *The Time Stream*

We believed that then. He forgot to breathe. I missed the unrelieved anxiety and hostility of his laughter, the breadth of his anger. Waves of light and leaves flowed around the house like a solar wind.

"How frail is beauty's doom," Mary Robinson, "Inscribed to Maria"

Dawn from a sickly sky

"inly stung"                         Aria
                                     Area

Not remembering you       Suite

The last individual. My favorite endangered species. Reintroducing him into the wild. The problem of his trusting everyone. He is lost in the wilderness of his work. He is relentlessly alone. We share this, as we do everything though it brings us no closer, divided as we are by our language.

You and with him

Face another face

The moon burst                  Like a rocket

Twin children at one time in a bookish garden. We were alone together in a small room or maybe a plane imagining the past. Unable to keep up the pretense of speaking. The words were the unreal part of the dream.

The reasonable universe       Implosion
                                     Rock fall
The leaves and the breeze

Kissed by                         This

"…self-prepared the splendid banquet stands / Self-poured the nectar sparkles in the bowl," Mary Tighe "Psyche." "The dead characters baffled me, and the phosphorescent decay outstripped my intellect."
John Taine, *The Time Stream*

His sun came out only at night. His work never stopped. We tied our knots and he continued in his thought. I sat with him. We talked and then sat in silence. He seemed sincere. His eyes were transparent in the light.

"Let me sing you // two yous, a shred," Taylor Brady, *Microclimates*

Two versions of what

restive but

"…Fire won't do it / the twin translation to another life," Gavin Selerie, "Danse Macabre"

"What did you want from me then?" he referred to a time in another city. I was traveling for a job but it was another job. "Can I touch you now?" he said from across the table. "But you already are," I said. We were an equal distance from each other. The world was a degree hotter. The equation was worked out. He was the government. I was the people. But that was then.

| According to his ability each | Affinity |
| | Duet |
| Not personal but human | Like breasts |

Through him like an accordion

Vatic trajectory                    *Song For* sung for

Mechanical breath

The planet dark around us. Hungry for our missed tea but unwilling to leave. All day waiting to speak. Constructing the afternoon around his stylized anger. "No ray of light falls on the darkness of your heart," Andrew Bird, "Pathetique." A banquet of possibility is spread out before us. Is physical. Is imminent or is already taking place.

The pattern is suspended around the woman creating it. She is involved in a conspiracy. The pattern is traditional. It is over her head. She has hung it there. Information is dense in the material. She can project the future with this form. Her method is not relational, though she exists in a complex fabric of social relationships, but is more interruptive.

I feel the music inside me

But the world is a threat

"Western I. Casting unecological shadow." Gail Scott, *My Paris*

He is lost in the music of his work. We are the largest consuming nation. We have to work out a future. You and me and I. A next step in our dance of death. He called his friends Deaths. Part of the burden of the past now electronically sloughed off.

The woman feels the sand in her hands. In her veins. The organization is warm against her skin and under her feet. There is a roar from a vent by her window where the whole city breathes. She tells herself to enjoy her exhaustion. People are imprisoned. In themselves. She is alive.

Does he support the organization? What is this business we are in together? These and other questions when we meet. Our connections strained beyond recognition. He is lost in the wilderness of his work. "Hard-won, self-acquired, self-earned property!" Karl Marx, *Das Kapital*. Our small talk deteriorates into chaos like an ecosystem about to tip.

"But what is supposed to rise from this collapse? Only their original, intimate dialogue." Brent Cunningham, *Bird & Forest*

His face is my face. Or mine is hers. It is a wholesale use of one by the other. There are objections. "It is important," she says, "to get used to the hunger." She is my twin as much as she is yours. Mine is the name of the moon in that system. The trajectories are interlocked. Our exchange is also lopsided. Like a cosmic event, it has the unevenness of personal talk.

Like statues the women are destroyed. They break. We break down. Into.

Dirge
The rocks
You taught
The disbelief


Our birthday again. Everything we can speak is between us all the time especially now. As I stand and you list. Your hard-won status as a dead poet is history but is not the only historical thing. "These knots you taught" and the portable aspects of what we do remain when there is no speech.

"Twin heads now lean, recontort," John Wilkinson, *Speaking Twins*. Finding out late about the third twin who will change everything. An electronic song or codebook sequence unravels our activity. Will the new configuration protect them? Us. Me. Zealous soldier of. All that we are. In all our twinned glory. Fortune. From what will.

Be known

Embattled ecstatic

Aporia
Our community
Subcontracted                    Villification

Testimonial                       Not

Last man standing

"The head and legs of the Buddha"

It's true she was the center of it then. The big lake of her face. Her words dying. The just outside of town thing. What used to be called a trip breaks down. The organization is in trouble. The landscape takes itself apart. Like a shot. Fast. Another old world word. Onward.

Into the valley of

Face to the wall

The war

That image destroyed

# Pure Lyric

Like pure war a politics and architecture. The ramparts are built to be destroyed. Arriving at another city the city remembered before us is just a name. The politics of working together. Of writing together including movement. Logistics. Only the form of our existence is left like a retinal pattern. An engagement. A list of our accomplishments composed of these notes coheres for a moment in local space.

There is an individual. Nobody helps him but nobody talks about it. The beds of the hotels when we were that lucky. Not a competition though someone wins. He uses me like he uses the other equipment. Simple repetition. I can't say what I would do. Or did. Or know.

# Arrhythmia

You and you again go
Returning as you do
Known or unknown
A thought as in temporal
Eternal as turning
Step away from the car

Both of us agree to be
You define yourself as
Named and as speaking
But what not said was
A pause in:
A soft schedule

Not calendarized
But frozen outside a miniature
But central ocean
Deepest lake
Survival means going
Mistaken as with any sudden
Forward jerk

I created myself to death
That said
Dying words
Wasn't in fact
What she said was
The next thought we walk
In our own blood

# Transformation of the Twins

Not going back
"something passes between two things…"
Hospital or moon
Forget the moon
"to feel oneself in heaven"
I have to go now
Gone along the edge road with
She as me in far off
Daily apocalypse but no judgment
No judgment but in
As if already done
But it was not like hell
An engraving
Together again before
The funeral before the war
Then I am the man
In this lake or womblike
Neighborhood of us
Two hungers enlarged
Unless and until
Ordinary hunger
You feed me with yourself

# No Moon

Old time synthesizer
Emotion ocean

Lean on the dial
Acoustic sunrise

Radio and sky the same claim
The same way back

Recorded laughter call-in host
Bubbling through the stratosphere

From your veins in blue trails
To your brain and back

Never going off duty claims
A direct channel

Fake moon
Nonunique finite and faithful

Animate schematic universe
Smart jump

At no time does it get better
Death and development

Our other new department
Existing fragmentation

Thinking-in-time
Visible all night

# My Scream

Today I am screaming in love
The water created by raining
For him to steal me and say
I have a song for your lovely street

The lavender moon where you want it to be
The water created by chiming
Strings in a circular pattern like rings
Like pebbles off the dock at the end of air

This will fall away you say
Today screaming in love I am
Not present but presence only naturally
Using something other than your name

To mean you in one word
Reflexively and before the end
Of the song we sing when we
On the street again with your lovely I have

To steel myself when people talk
It is as if they are singing
Why do you rise in your purple thing?
What is it that a moon can mean?

Not round but straight
Not soft but soft what moon now
With its light me after all this
Mere heat entering my heart

Who do you love and what
Do you know about that sweet anything
You are not telling me repetition
I don't already know?

# From *A Tonalist*

# 1. Spectrum's Rhetoric

Light changes the sentence. A subject persists in memory sounding. Walks along the edge of the continent. Tea leaves piled like seaweed in a cup in a mind pink on the inside and like the sea dark. Cut orchids and peonies as writing or going out. Green of stems. Green of the sea. A long drive. A longer walk. Movement is aloud.

"It is just this moment of red mind..." Dōgen, *Shobogenzo*

You as an address various and specific know where you are. Who you are. But what do I know? "What do I know and when did I know it?" you ask later. More on that.

A hill looms like a wave of earth. El Cerrito goes down to the sea, the bay, nearby. The hill intimated by the name is in Albany. Here. In California. Goes to the sea. In green. The sea white.

The city in the distance
Surrounded by

Color drains from it as light recedes but the color remains in this Western version. This version of the West. That being the point (of light visible as) (it is) made complicated by the physicality of thought.

"the circumstances
like a fabric ripping
inside the body"

Norma Cole, *a little a & a*

But what is the West? What is light? What is empire? What color? The body as light as perceived from the inside out. The arrangement of color. The arrangement of time. Local time. Thought as action. For time and color's sake. As read. Among the hills golden and yet not empirical or not merely so or empirical and yet not empire, though of it. But what happened?

"I saw the
countryside

for seconds like
a film thru"

George Albon, *Empire Life*

What happens to make us believe what we see. To see what we read as being read we write in color.

"Our best research is left with its mouth open."

Reading a diary backwards. Writing it. Writing the experience before having it. Thinking of an indistinct town from a distance. Of the city. Thinking about the war in a store in the midst of the empire. Thinking about Cornell, not the boxes but the diary. The lack of sentimentality in his Romantic Museum—or the mad presence of sentiment. Or its ephemerality.

In Eisenstein's *Romance Sentimental* a woman plays a black piano in black and then a white one in white. She sings an old song of longing. Handwritten explosions come later after the branches rush by and the sea is included. There are monsters.

"I may forever lose the light…" Kamau Brathwaite, *Zea Mexican Diary*. "If she should die…I may forever lose the light the light — the open doors"

Aspens like sequins (for example)
Unlike lichen
An arrested splash

198

Green and light green
Or black with white
The lichen yellow and black

"I don't know where you buy it or whether there is a premium for
buying it. I don't understand how to do it or use it."

*The Lotus Sutra*

The body in its place
Hybrid of door and face
Present text to be
As you are there then where
Transcripted in its entire
Repetition each day
More patient than anyone
The act of
Who speaking moves
Gives her notes away

"The act of remembering or the vibrations of the sutra
Crash though the real world"

Philip Whalen, "Four Other Places"

We see to the bottom of the lake. The stems deep among white rocks.
Green and red leaves flat on the black water. Green to yellow. Yellow
lotus buds. Leaves furled. Magenta inside. Spread out on the lake. Blue
now of the sky. Black and green of trees. Beauty of husband nearby.
Lotus and trees in the background. Husband. Half lake half sky.

Untitled

Mariposa lily

Black and white

Lotus ubiquitous there (East) as here the cross. (West.) It is not about death, suffering or sacrifice, but about cultivation, recitation, transcription, translation, genre, gender switching, mud and light. The bright things that grow there.

Darkly

But silent

Stance

Among the Buddhas in my mother's album is the wooden one in Berkeley Zen Center pictured with a vase of columbines, a candle and a small statue of Kwannon. The altar for our wedding. And here we are kissing.

Years missing

Intervene when

Startled from sleep by the wind, I see again the peripheral beings I have lately noticed but who I can't see if I look directly at them. Rows of monks. Known to be Western monks. Rows of pale green robes. Green monks. Eastern but Western. Yellow lotus.

Merely a phenomenon of sight.

The house alight. Water on the floor. The house is empty or needs to be emptied. The room is filled with glasses, keys, keyboards, pillows and cups. It is dark. There are too many bright things. There was a party. A wake. Cabinets are open and broken. What can we do with this place? What are we doing here?

Hereinafter

Things given

Come back

The glass elephant in the painting of the lilacs floating in the photo like a thought over the three of us, my aunt, my mother and I on a couch. My mother's eyes, as if to say "Okay. What the hell. Here I am alive."

"I hold you like a river."
Esther Tellerman, "Mental Ground," translated by Keith Waldrop

Like heaven falling, the long line of cloud heads directly for us. It spills over our hill in slow motion. We see the fog in shreds above and descending. Next day we watch as it lightens and dissolving, we pull away.

Wandering at the bottom of the ocean of air, reading two slim volumes. One a translated revelation, the other about the weather.

"And I saw a new sky and a new earth."
Revelations 21:1, Revelations 20:11

"And books were opened"
Bleeding meaning
Body in time
Just as we said (read)
Red thinking but not
Speaking though speaking
Enough to say

Bleeding meaning in a hospital on Earth sitting—a skinny Buddha with good hair. I meet your famous friends and say Tonalism with you and you say "Good." "Title." We agree right there referring to past and future with sweeping gestures. You point to windowlight with the hand you have making

"The highest heaven in the world of forms form"

The painter in the painting. The gray clouds of paint behind the mailboxes like her smoke. The black trees. Her signature in the corner. Legible. I did this.

The name affixed I see

Drains the life

Roars into me from another world

But that painting is unsigned. The autograph is in my mind. This is not my mother. These are not our mailboxes. They are in the country, in fact, in the clouds. Ours were on the base, by the house, on a street. I can't remember them. I can't read this.

People with colors

Arrive and grieve They leave

The receptacles Have left

Petals scattered

Old sunlight. Morning fire. She dreams that she speaks. The lines of the sea. The distance is complete. The creek swollen. Oaks with moss hung. The sweep of light from the lighthouse as approaching on Highway 1. Lens, headlight, windowlight. The trees braided impossibly upward. A gold rectangle on transparent blue. Thickly pictured. The lens was invented by a French physicist. This was his room. This his bed we sleep in. This *we.*

"The landscape
is the portrait of
the sun. Only
skin is skin deep."

Norma Cole, *Spinoza in Her Youth*

I can hear as well as see the quiet as you sound it in your mind. Is it
my imagination? Is it your speech? A change occurs during the sound.
The colors are audible. The sea disappears into the afternoon through
a line of gray leafed blue gum. The green is green. The light dark. The
artificial log burns down. Books, notebooks and I reflect like television
in the glass doors of the fire. Reading (watching) Alan Halsey's *Memory
Screen*. Fire sucked by wind. We take the measure of it. Screen and
wind and I. Read him. Read you.

Lyric intimate of
Eucalyptus

The green countryside
Comes out of my head

Writes as taken
"I was taken"

The green (me)
Surrounds (you)

Each of the characters rests on a lotus. There are slight variations
in the flowers. The late sun makes the rocks seem young. For now
we will remember everything in advance. I never knew this was the
beach of that dream. The cove of that love.

Are we different from the sun? Seeing the rocks through the sea like
a window to the present. "Renunciation of fame, fortune, power and
security." Why not? Why do we want what we want? What do we do?

203

We are not lyric but transitional. Not sun but sung. Not color but of color. A flock of crows standing sounds. Or gulls. A row of rows. "Bowing to the Buddha while being annoyed by demons."

Basalt foam and
Rocks clapping
Damp sand and saw grass
Occluded trail
Jet like transparent meteor
Wave by wave
Roar of highway

Strong tea to hand
Tangled ganglia
Tops of trees
Things thoughtful here
Sun suddenly
Next day same fire same trees
Reading Niedecker
Spreads herself out on a field

"A good map will represent most of a lifetime's fieldwork."
Oliver Morton, *Mapping Mars*

What is Tonalism or as often—so-called Tonalism? Did it exist even when it existed? Can an idea of it be used to think about a contemporary phenomenon in writing? A Tonalist thinking. Originally there was an emphasis on color, on a monochromatic approach and landscape. The person is the color of the landscape and is lit. There is a sense, a sensing, of light during transitional times of the day, transition itself, a muted but glowing experience of color. Craft as in the act of bending waves through time. The activity is precise.

The image is saturated with absence if, as most often, there is no figure. Or if a figure is present it is alone. Or if various figures are present as with Xavier Martinez's *Apache Dance* which depicts a bar in Paris—women and men incandescent—the figures alone together, their backs to us, something between them besides light. Not landscape but just escape. The movement of the mind through color and time. Working through the didactic into the seductive. Decorative as in pattern for its own sake—repetitive, emblematic, literal, local, but generalist in its sense of locale. Not the snapshot but the establishing shot. California. Drama of air, light, water and color. An emphasis on light, for which read sound. Color is sounded.

"No, it is not a collage. Hell flowers." (Spicer) "What you call collage I call thinking." (Halsey)

Gottardo Piazzoni's Tonalist obsession with the moon. Going to the top of an East Bay hill to view it with his family, cheering as it rises.

"[A]lways with the sense of mystery and savagery that appear to mark the artist's work." Thus Lucy B. Jerome orientalizes Xavier Martinez in the San Francisco *Call*. Martinez was a prodigy. He asserted his Mexican and Indian heritage in his painting and his writing. Did he think of himself as Lucy thought of him? Or as Tonalist—or as A Tonalist--in being not the nonspecific person but one saturated with color with subjectivity, identity, physicality, sex, race, health, age. Rage.

James McNeill Whistler, the erstwhile grandfather of Tonalism, once wandered by Martinez painting in a Paris museum and said something like, "Good job." But the A Tonalist posited here is irreconcilable with Whistler's arrangements, his whitist "art for art's sake." His arrangements in white, women in white, symphonies in white. His infamous mother (arrangement in gray and black), his Irish lover (purple and rose), later discarded for his whitist wife. This patriarch of that old Tonalism commented that "the future of art is in the hands of women," but he was so obviously, as they say, a hound. He was musical (with his terms) and ambitious. Vicious with both men and women. Ripper connection. More on that. "You also, our first great" (Ezra

Pound, "To Whistler, American"). "Show us there's a chance of at least winning through." Or not winning. Not that. But this. These.

"Magnificent pink roses, chrysanthemums in a Greek vase, the color spectrum's rhetoric in an untranslated book, apocalyptic wallpaper for the classroom. Patience. There is a comet tail, a yellowish drip of unconscious brush stroke to the right. Have a drink. Blackness is before you and black is your favorite color. Honk. A customer will haul the installation away. Even now this gravedigger cruises on an ocean liner. He teeters on the edge of your work. Objects unrecognize you. The East is empty, there is nothing left to the West except the past, which is groundless night, a mass solution (like panic) to solitude, an imperishable escape. Let's go to Paris. Let's live, therefore we'll think. We'll be admitted to the best seats at the Opera, indicted for treason, encouraged to seduce our new enemies, become diplomats, say grace with trackless courtesans. There are dull beatitudes and reanimated brains. Houdini. The art of dissemination is the sign of the prodigy."

Jerry Estrin, "Citizen's Dash," *Rome, A Mobile Home*

The inward present. The indefinite maintained as a kind of discipline. Abstract simplification. Not arcane and yet there is a suggestive darkness. A realism of forms which melt into each other. Spiritual realism in which spiritual is defined as a formal practice relating to a belief in love but not of a person. Or of a person. And realism is verisimilitude in drag.

A finely dissonant harmony asserts a relentless quietism. Luminist white rock, another white and black as if written, still another darker white with green lines and areas of lighter green like land masses. Black like the sea.

Not a movement so much as a mood, an orientation, a realization that much that seemed forbidden is in fact required. Doubt, for example, especially self-doubt. A man can be in love with his equivocation. He can be equivocal about his doubt. He can use his knowledge against himself.

"Choked with interval of ecstatic doubt"
Andrew Joron, "Anima, Macula," *The Removes*

It is the beginning of the century. There is war all around. There is an empire. New media dominate the age, changing the old, replicating patterns of thought outward until they are discernable only to those morbidly sensitive to pattern. Information migrates. People are left behind in the wars.

Pont Neuf from below. Xavier Martinez. His life in Paris. Yellow light. Dark silhouette of a man, mist and smoke. The sky is the color of the meditation wall. Five points of light, one of reflection.

Hazing over during the drive
Actual bridge remembered trees
Remembered islands and streets

Glow on the western horizon. Clarity of sky drained of color after steady movement through the point out into the bay and back. White against darker white.

Wingspan pictured
While the wall resting
Into itself and the purple
Remains of the storm and spring
Feeds the pond deepens
Swarms with tadpoles
We in the mud go beyond
And up into the cliff
And forest meadow
Great Blue Heron

Black and white reduces everything to tone. There is no color but
color. There is light and dark. Heron bent as stands, folding up. Time
and light again. "Thanks to our ability to stop we are able to observe."

Thich Nhat Hahn, *Breath! You are Alive!*

Not stopping but going out into
Inner reaches of San Pablo Bay
Point Pinole was Giant Station
Another East Bay dynamite factory
Always blowing up
Oceanic perspective
Pebbles to rock and back again
Eucalyptus, bay laurel, evergreen and oak
Large remnants of the world on the beach
As if after the war as if
The war were ever over

Only the objections
Rusting toxic ghost fleet
On its way despite
Were ever over
Our belief in that ocean

Faint with color
I have seen you
Faced with color
Glazed successively through which light
Penetrates and is reflected back
As a formal relationship or
Paradise cult boundary
The letter (your letter)
Between heaven and earth
Anything could have happened
But the particle stays fixed
Space and time fluctuate around it

(You don't die)
To be a fact is to
Reason from the bottom up
The old problem of telling time at night
"Forget subject matter," they say
"Forgotten," we reply but it's a trick

And again dreaming a phrase

Time and light
Having gone on
Because alive
Drenched with

Dawn after green lit dawn
Or goes down
Whose bombs fall
Into the muddy world
Whose time goes on

Alexander Helwig Wyant, Tonalist, had a stroke at 42 while traveling out West. His right hand was paralyzed. He taught himself to paint with his left hand. It is a somewhat looser technique. He was known for the fluid brush and restrained palette he came to from the Barbizon school. He died in '92.

Sixteen breathing exercises
Four establishments of mind
Body, feelings, mind and objects of mind
"looking deeply to shed light"

"336 symmetries, the highest possible number for a surface of genus three…The Eightfold Way in marble is divided into seven-sided patches" that one can feel to exist as rubbing they continuously change into each other and also

Fringed blossoms of eucalyptus
Tulip trees, oak and acacias

Objects and events at the origin

Well inside the body
Memory with desire

Not the sea
The sight of the sight of the sea

The body seeing sight
Seeing scent

"Scent

     the simple

         the perfect

order

   of that flower

       water lily"

Lorine Niedecker, "North Central"

One claims light
The other dark and yet

Seem to be the same
Statement because arranged

As parallel universes do exist
For example yours and mine

Like beams that won't meet
Until space curves or time ends

There is never any time
Even now it seems gone

As we fall bodily from line
To line it is quiet

The sound of my head in your voice
Each word alone with the other

Sounded out as in
I should have told you

Once more from the top
Nothing is what I wanted

# From *Divination*

# Transposition

Not the question of who
Is legible to whom or who
Counts or the diagram
Of that sentence commuted
But what is (trans) sent
Are they real he asked
Real expensive she said
But it was an episode
Not the real poetry
Addresses
The list of which gets
What does it get again?
Is there a transposition
When sound imitates music?
As Duncan wrote
He loved Levertov
In the letters
That make love
Evolve as a consequence
Of telling
What is human swells
What burns red What is
Sound remains strong
Or lists
As when the list
Addresses changes of
Who is read and what is known
That she was a witch
Or just another poet
Eligible for scorn
A sentiment transposed into
Resentment in the best sense

As resent means
Send again to see
Direction as reckoning
Grammar to glamour
Red to end spectrum to
Speculative poetics to a subset
Of text and hex
Violet to violent
"Even as we are most 'sent'"
Letters to love (hers)
Unknown to renown finally
Revealed to (be) each other

# Our Rage

As if poetry had a place

The word hotel

A downward spiral occurs

Our rage takes us away

Clock wasted

Pillow ticking

Your head on it for days

For hours mine

The hotel foreign

The argument a joke

Our rage the same

I won't go without knowing

You say and then you know

# "Welcome Dear Chaos"

## (Michael McClure, from *Plum Stones*)

Vexed from the start the zephyr
Question unlocked the highly
Polished box unleashing a torrent
Down which anyone would hesitate
To drop though drop we did
Elbow by toe by fist by thumb
Ending up hum down hanging by
A shoestring kissed by flame leaf
By gold crushed into the applesauce
Inevitable once the butterfly
Wing released the chaos theory we lived
Or died by nothing was left but to
Bark at the dream or begin again

Thumb to fist as if only when we start does
The question of the flame torrent
Down the fist of its bark becomes known
To us though to hum was enough to
Make applesauce into gold and let
The butterfly escape the thumb of
The chaosophist, the leaf to wing
Into the dream to polish the zephyr
Until nothing is left but a drop
Or a shoestring and to elbow
Or toe remains the only way out

There were more wings and more cards. The leaves in the cream were iridescent. They were inevitable and venerable like Holmes himself. Moriarty was missing. Everyone was suspicious and resistant. No one could keep track of the results. The address was clear. It was like me to you only not. The phrase "fellow visionaries" was an accusation. You were the accused, the accursed.

Zephyr she screamed but too late
He like a leaf elbow over toe had
To wing along drop by drop
A shoestring away from flame
He put his fist down the thumb of the
Butterfly answering the question
Of how to begin hum or dream as gold
As possible while not forgetting to polish
The torrent with the applesauce of desire

But there was no polish to the dream of lists
Other than what was toe up or fist down
She was like a butterfly to me or other bug
Wing, hum, flame she had it all
I can't speak about the applesauce but of
The zephyr I can go on in torrents
The question was the start the focus
The other side of the card where the shoestring
Was arranged by thumb to invoke the bark
Of drop drop drop where the elbow is the
Throat of the leaf set to begin on time

Applesauce was nothing to me then
Chaos thumbs the hum off the zephyr
The unspoken torrent becomes the question
The leaf gold the butterfly flame the drop dream until
Finally the applesauce and so on


Overwhelmed with clues, Holmes comes home. Words dance in his head like men. Everything is evidence of something. Counterintuitively, the problem on the game board does not repeat. There is in memory the expectation of the symmetricality of events, but there is nothing on either side of the cards that would allow us to believe in such a result. The impossible becomes the only alternative when the possible is eliminated. The game is afoot (toe or thumb) but this zephyr is an ill wind if there ever was one. It's raining again in the wordland.

Using 27 words supplied by
Bruce Conner in 1975 in
response to a request for words
made in sending him the
text of "Waking From Sleep a
Thousand Miles Thick"